ENCOUNTERS WITH TADEUSZ KANTOR

'Theatre is the finest of the fine arts, because it resides between art and life'

Tadeusz Kantor

This unique set of reminiscences, written by one of the actors who worked closely with Kantor over a long period of time, ranges from the anecdotal to the theoretical. Kantor's work offers some of the most disconcerting allegories of Modernism and a quintessential expression of the unconscious during a bitter period of human history. Kantor's stern but affectionate guardianship of his troupe of travelling players comes off Miklaszewski's pages with warmth, humanity and humour.

Kryzstof Miklaszewski is a major figure in the world of contemporary Polish cultural life and for thirteen years, between 1973 and 1986, was an actor in Kantor's theatre. A presenter of arts programmes for Polish television, Miklaszewski has also directed numerous significant documentary films of theatrical and artistic activities. He is currently Artistic Director of the Theatre Rampa in Warsaw.

The translator and editor, George Hyde, lived and taught in Poland during and after the communist period. He is the author of numerous essays on Polish life and letters, also of several books and essays on Modernist writers, and translates from Polish and Russian. He recently retired as Professor of English and Comparative Literature at Kyoto Women's University, Japan, and is now Senior Research Fellow at the University of East Anglia, where he is writing books on David Storey and George Borrow.

ENCOUNTERS WITH TADEUSZ KANTOR

Krzysztof Miklaszewski

Edited and translated by
George Hyde

Routledge
Taylor & Francis Group

LONDON AND NEW YORK

First published in paperback 2005
First published in hardback 2002
by Routledge
2 Park Square, Milton Park, Abingdon, Oxon, OX14 4RN

Simultaneously published in the USA and Canada
by Routledge
270 Madison Ave, New York, NY, 10016

Routledge is an imprint of the Taylor & Francis Group

Typeset in Stempel Garamond by M Rules
Printed and bound in Great Britain by
MPG Books Ltd., Bodmin, Cornwall

British Library Cataloguing in Publication Data
A catalogue record for this book is available from the British Library

Library of Congress Cataloging in Publication Data
Miklaszewski, Krzysztof.
Encounters with Tadeusz Kantor/Krzysztof Miklaszewski;
edited and translated by George Hyde.
p. cm. — (Polish and East European theatre archive; 8)
Includes index.
1. Kantor, Tadeusz, 1915—Criticism and interpretation.
I. Hyde, G.M. (George M.), 1941-II. Title. III. Series.

PN2859.P66 K367 2002
792'.0233'092—dc21
2001048190

ISBN 0-415-37263-1 (limp)
ISBN 0-415-27032-4 (cased)

In memory of my mother,
to whom I (Krzysztof Miklaszewski)
also owe my discovery of . . . Cricot

Tadeusz Kantor. Photo: Wojciech Kryński

CONTENTS

LIST OF PLATES

INTRODUCTION TO THE SERIES

The *Polish and East European Theatre Archive* makes available English translations of dramatic literature as well as monographs and informative studies on playwrights, theatre artists, theatres and stage history. Although emphasis is placed on the contemporary period, the *Polish and East European Theatre Archive* also encompasses the nineteenth-century roots of modern theatre practice in romanticism and symbolism. The individual plays will contain authoritative introductions that place the works in their historical and theatrical contexts.

Daniel Gerould

ACKNOWLEDGEMENTS

The author wishes to thank Robert Robertson without whom this book would not have been possible. His involvement as a contributor, facilitator and consultant played a key role throughout.

A special thanks go to Małgorzata Czerwińska whose patience and tireless efforts helped the author along the way.

The translator wishes to thank the University of East Anglia, United Kingdom, and the World Literature Department of the University of Vilnius, Lithuania, for making research time and facilities available.

Every effort has been made to trace the ownership of all copyright material in this book. In the event of any questions about the use of any material, the author, while expressing regret for any inadvertent error, will be happy to make the necessary acknowledgement in future printings.

TRANSLATOR'S PREFACE

At first sight, the title given by Krzysztof Miklaszewski to his invaluable book of reminiscences, interviews, theatrical texts, photographs, travel notes, descriptions, and evocations, seems misleading. How can a man who lived so close to the subject of his study, a member of the "family" as it were, speak of his "encounters" with him? Was Miklaszewski not one of Kantor's "stars", as well as a friend, and the author of a superb video recording of the lessons of the master? Why the distance the term "spotkanie" (meeting, encounter) implies? Why not "working with Kantor", or "on the road with Kantor", or "behind the scenes with Kantor"? Or why not simply "a critical biography" of the life and work of a creative artist the author evidently understood inside and out, possessing an insight and empathy which cannot fail to impress the reader with its authenticity and immediacy?

There is, of course, a reason, and it has to do with the quintessential qualities of Kantor's work, and a profound and passionate conviction about the invulnerability of these qualities, which Miklaszewski's method soon manages to communicate. Kantor, who lived among his theatrical "family" on a day-to-day basis, was nevertheless a deeply lonely man, whose solitariness is his real theme. Kantor was also a sceptical man, for whom the business of theatre, the world of the arts generally, the public presentation of private experience, was shot through with fatal compromises. Kantor, eloquent as he was, as these interviews show, distrusted words, since words have parted company with the things they represent, especially in our age of propaganda and communication industries (which may be only a more refined kind of propaganda). For Kantor, a brush-stroke or a wooden plank spoke volumes, where volumes of texts fell silent. He reached for words like a painter reaching for his brush and his paint. Kantor's work, in other words, resists continuous narration.

Moreover, Kantor was one of the last great Dadas of art: by which I mean that chance, *objets trouvés*, equivocal spaces, the deconstructed structures of contemporary reality, dreams and displacements, all speak louder than words when he is around. Dada is above all a gesture of refusal, of subversion (subverting even itself), of denial and defiance. Dada can't be bought, summed up, interpreted or transcribed: it just *is*; and it is particularly restless in the company of large "finished" texts. Miklaszewski's method in writing his book approximates in some respects to Kantor's own way of generating texts: by cutting and pasting, mincing and wrapping, exploding and pastiching the fragments – as in a kaleidoscope – are shaken up and fall differently into patterns which are always intriguingly new. He is always conscious of his obligation to *mediate*; but he does not let this contractual obligation interfere for too long with the crucial element of surprise. You think you are reading one thing, for example, a travelogue, and suddenly you are reading another, for example, a sort of Kierkegaardian *Either/Or* or *Fear and Trembling*.

There is an element of clowning here in Miklaszewski's book, as in Kantor, but restrained; a delighted, childlike discovery, as in Kantor; an obsessive, childlike probing, as in Kantor. I have chosen to translate the Polish word "spotkanie" as "encounter", despite the fact that its first meaning is "meeting", because I want it (legitimately!) to have the existential and aesthetic resonance which "encounter" catches, and maybe communicate the passion which, lurking just off the page, links Miklaszewski and Kantor in a bond of love and death, just as it links Kantor and the authors whose texts he cuts up.

Clichés theatre historians love to use about the "retreat from the word" in modernist theatre crumble into dust in the face of Kantor's passionate vision. The landscape of his plays is strewn with literary texts, literary symbols, literary characters (drawn from writers including Schulz, Witkacy, and Gombrowicz); but they are all subdued by his Dantesque vision of pain, death, carnival, and (postponed) redemption. With an additional urbanity, ease, and scrupulousness, Miklaszewski remains true to this vision at levels high and low, which his encounters carefully and tactfully suggest rather than denominate. He shares Kantor's fear and suspicion of cliché. But he also knows how to throw up a smokescreen when he needs to: as, indeed, does his Master. It was a useful accomplishment in "People's Poland": it is anywhere, for that matter.

Kantor was one of the great "translators" of modern and postmodern times, in the sense that he built the kind of symbolic arcades used by Walter Benjamin, cutting off a space in which we can talk with the dead. The task of the translator, confronted by Kantor, is, above all, to hold back, and to let language speak through him, disclosing its "futurity" as it does so. I have therefore approached Miklaszewski's text as respectfully as possible, even as some kind of poem, and as if its components fitted tightly together with a special kind of logic. At the same time, I have kept one eye firmly fixed on the communicative functions of translation, and I am convinced that these two aspects can never really be mutually exclusive for very long.

The point here is that Kantor's writings about theatre have only recently "encountered" translators worthy of them, who demonstrate a respectful sense of what Kantor is trying to say. Some of the earlier versions, especially the more ephemeral by-products of particular stagings, emanating mainly from Poland, have played a large part in contributing to the English sense of Polish drama – maybe of Polish culture generally – as wild, pretentious, and obscure. There is no denying the riotous elements of farce, carnival, parade, and circus in Kantor. These are as intrinsic to his seriousness as they are in the work of another great artist whom he resembles, Federico Fellini; nor the vertiginous mingling of these things with last rites, crucifixions, orgies, and execrations, again as in Fellini's case. But just as in Kantor's theatre, so in his, and Miklaszewski's, texts, a split-second timing, an unfailing taste and tact, a constructivist passion for form, and a strange, formalist purity of effect, work within and against the proliferating demons that inhabit his Dantean under-worlds. Kantor's translators, and Miklaszewski's, have to know this, and to strive for economy and precision in contexts which initially seem flatly to rule out the possibility of their existence. This gestural precision is what makes Kantor's work therapeutic rather than psychotic, and what allows him to share his dreams of evil with his audience, using the same uncanny, sharp-edged clarity as the great Polish artist Malczewski,[1] whose work he admired so much, and learned so much from. It is an exacting task: but then the task of the translator is always exacting, when the texture of the translation *matters*, as it always does with literature and the arts.

As for Miklaszewski himself, he is currently one of the luminaries of the cultural section of Polish television, and he has lost none of his flair for imaging and imagining. The way Miklaszewski introduces himself in the opening pages of his book tells us a lot about cultural Kraków, and provides a nicely contrasted context for Kantor's remorseless avant-gardism. But above all, he has what Kantor had: strange to find oneself borrowing, in this context, from D. H. Lawrence; but this shared thing was the Lawrencean fascination with the intermingled waters of the "river of life", and those of the "river of dissolution". Modern, moderner, modernity, modernist, modernest: Kantor goes forward as he goes back to the sources.

G. M. Hyde

Notes

1   Jacek Malczewski (1854–1929) was a major Symbolist painter who, in the words of the brochure accompanying his Barbican exhibition (London, 10 May to 8 July, 1990) had a "compelling vision which closely links his country's struggle for independence with his own search for identity": not necessarily in that order. For historical reasons, an interest in Poland's "struggle for independence" has sometimes led to a critical obfuscation of Malczewski's startling, deranged eroticism and cool dicing with death, as was shown in Miklaszewski's fine documentary, *Kantor on Malczewski – Personal Vision*, which accompanied the exhibition.

1. Krzysztof Miklaszewski as the Beadle in *Dead Class*.
Photo: Jacek Barcz

INTRODUCTION

I first heard about Tadeusz Kantor at home as a child. Home, to me, was Flat 8 on Studencka Street in Kraków. On the walls, next to some seventeenth-century French engravings, was the realist *Shoemakers' Monday* by Wacław Koniuszko,[1] pictures by Pronaszko,[2] Jan and Bolesław Cybis,[3] Jan's wife Hannah Rudzka-Cybisowa, and Maria Jarema,[4] recognised soon after her death as Poland's best abstract artist. Alongside sketches by Józef Chełmoński[5] and Juliusz Kossak[6] were watercolours by Nikifor of Krynica, the best of the Polish "Sunday painters." Guests at our table included doctors and oarsmen, such as Verey and Ustupski, the aforementioned Jarema, sculptor Jacek Puget[7] – heir to the native tradition of a "family school of painting" – the well-known writer Kornel Filipowicz, and Jarema's husband, Andrzej Stopka,[8] a typical *montagnard* who had married the daughter of splendid genre painter Wincenty Wodzinowski. Wodzinowski made a name for himself as one of the most creative Polish scenographers; one of his paintings still takes up half of the drawing-room wall. And then there was Uncle Władysław Józef Dobrowolski, polyglot and pedagogue, collector and animator, theatre historian and champion of many artistic causes. It was Władysław, along with Jarema's brother Józef, who called into being the Dada theatre "Cricot", which took everyone by storm in the thirties.

The name Cricot stuck in my mind very early on, especially since my mother (already a doctor of repute and later an actress in the Cricot theatre) had patiently explained to me the origins of the name.[9]

Cricot 2, on the other hand, I encountered only in 1969 when Stanisław Balewicz, family friend and indefatigable impresario of artistic life in Kraków, lured me into his Krzysztofory[10] for Witkacy's play *The Water Hen*. A production using techniques drawn from the art of the "happening", it lodged in my mind forever. This was my first encounter with Cricot 2.

I only managed to talk to Kantor himself for the first time three years later, when theatre critic Marian Sienkiewicz decided to produce a new journal, and asked me to interview the Master for the first issue. Kantor had just come back from Paris, where he had produced Witkacy's *The Shoemakers* with a French group.

This meeting led to some rapid developments. As head of the editorial board of the theatrical section of Kraków Television, I decided to produce some documentaries showing the famous director at work. *The Anatomy of a Performance* recorded the different stages of the birth of a single production, and involved the director being on camera from the first rehearsal to the first public performance. Kantor, who was in the grip of his concept of "The Impossible Theatre", was at that time, in 1972–1973, just beginning work on Witkacy's play *Lovelies and Dowdies*.[11] This was how the first Polish film about Cricot 2, *Tadeusz Kantor's Cloakroom*, came about. It wasn't to be shown until four years later. But the film was very well received and sold to several countries; Kantor also gave his enthusiastic approval.

It was my fate to follow in the footsteps of my late mother, Jadwiga Dobrowolska, and become an actor. I accompanied Kantor from 1973 until a memorable series of appearances in Argentina in 1987, and became committed to presenting these encounters with Kantor's art to my readers . . .

Notes

1   Wacław Koniuszko (1854–1900) was an artist who depicted interiors of houses in the Kraków region and Jewish backstreets, as well as the lives of craftsmen.

2   The Pronaszko brothers, Andrzej (1888–1961) and Zbigniew (1885–1958), were co-founders (with Tytus Czyżewski) of the formist movement in Polish art. Formism was a Polish version of constructivism. Andrzej worked extensively in the theatre along constructivist lines; he also made use of real objects in symbolic contexts à la Kantor. Zbigniew was also a formist and scenographer, but then pursued an academic career in Kraków.

3   Jan Cybis (1897–1972) was a post-impressionist colourist remembered also for his editorial work and *Painter's Notebook*.
    Bolesław Cybis (1895–1957) had a more striking, surreal style of painting, combining (like de Chirico) distorted dream-like space-times and archaic and exotic subjects, frequently erotic.
    Hanna Rudzka-Cybisowa (1897–1984), wife of Jan, was also a colourist, and professor of the Academy of Fine Arts in Kraków. She invited Kantor to work as a professor in the Academy but in 1968 he was expelled during the wave of anti-semitism action.

4   Maria Jarema (Jaremianka) (1908–1958) was associated with the Kraków group of experimental and innovative artists. She was a sculptor, painter and designer for the Cricot theatre. She used bold yet very precise lines, as well as child-like blocks and stripes of colour, which give her paintings a fascinating texture. Her sculptures recall Brancusi.

5   Józef Chełmoński (1849–1914), combines realist landscape painting with what the well-known Polish art historian Tadeusz Dobrowolski calls "an epic kind of poetry". Chełmoński was one of the biggest influences on traditionalist Polish art.

6   Juliusz Kossak (1824–1899) was one of the most popular painters of his time as a result of his vivid, patriotic, old Polish themes. He worked in water colours a great deal, and to some extent illustrated the historical literature of his time, especially the Nobel Prizewinner Henryk Sienkiewicz.

7   Jacek Puget (1904–1977) is recorded in Tadeusz Dobrowolski's *Sztuka Krakowa* as a "sculptor with an exceptional sense of form and material", and was an impressionist realist, several of whose busts are particularly noteworthy. A member of Cricot, actor and dancer.

8   Andrzej Stopka (1904–1973) was an *informel* artist of the Kraków Group, and co-founder of the Stage Design Department in the Kraków Academy of Fine Arts.

9   As Kantor took pleasure in explaining more than once, the odd name Cricot is an anagram of "to cyrk" ("this (or that) is a circus"). This links high and low art, the proscenium arch and the Big Top; but especially important, evidently, was the childhood image of the kind of Russian shrove-tide fair Stravinsky celebrated in *Petrushka*, when he found his own exotic versions of the *Commedia dell' Arte* characters there.

10 The gallery, one of Kraków's splendid ancient cellars, is still functioning as an art gallery of the Kraków Group (plus an amiable coffee bar) close to the centre of the city. The Kraków Modern Artists Group was formed as a result of the political thaw which followed the

death of Stalin in October 1956. The group included such names as Jaremianka, Kantor, Stopka, Puget. Here in the Krzysztofory Gallery, Kantor held his Cricot 2 rehearsals. All first night performances up to *Dead Class* were also held here.

11 Stanisław Ignacy Witkiewicz's play *Lovelies and Dowdies* (*Nadobnisie i Koczkodany*) is also known under the title *Dainty Shapes and Hairy Apes*.

2. The author of the book as Kantor's actor. Photo: Jacek Barcz

3. Tadeusz Kantor. Photo: Wojciech Kryński

1

THE LEGISLATOR AND THE
RENOVATOR OF RADICAL IDEAS

Kantor talked so much about the past that he seemed to be repeating Norwid's well-known formula: "The past is today, but a bit further off."[1]

Kantor used to say, "I draw upon tradition." He was constantly invoking his Polish forebears. He proclaimed: "I always try to reveal the whole context of my art." He cried: "Artists who maintain that they have thought up everything in their art for themselves are either swindlers or . . . idiots."

And then, in a rage directed simultaneously at his fascinated audience and at himself, absolutely in control and in one breath, he would let loose all the keywords of his artistic origins: Kraków – Frycz – Pronaszko[2] – Witkacy – Schulz – Gombrowicz – Dada – Duchamp – cyrk, or circus – Cricot. It is worth trying to reconstruct the significance of this list of names.

Kraków, for Kantor, was always the real City of Art, in which history had constantly made its claims felt; claims that became imprisoned and entombed, but a city which had witnessed some of art's most significant revolutions – at least as far as Polish art is concerned. Karol Frycz, a "citizen of the world" and artist who spanned three different Polish epochs, and Andrzej Pronaszko, the eternal revolutionary of theatrical form (for many years the closest associate of Leon Schiller), were Kantor's teachers: first in the Kraków School of Fine Art, and then in the Kraków theatre and the living tradition of Witkiewicz.

The great Polish trinity of Witkacy, Schulz and Gombrowicz, who have only recently been recognised and canonised by the West were, for a young art student from the Małopole provinces, incomparable models for sustained study; as were the Dadaists of the Cabaret Voltaire. The atmosphere of Kraków, the perspective of Frycz, the radicalism of Pronaszko – all great creative innovators – left an indelible imprint on the memory of the artist in formation. And then there was, in addition, the significant Kraków Dada episode that the first Cricot embodied, which one of its creators, Józef Jarema, defined in the following terms:

> The Cricot group was founded on the initiative of painters: which is to say that the specific expressive form of Cricot's theatricality is the powerful element of *plastic art in the staging* . . . The action on stage is apprehended above all *visually*. The eye is the main agent of our perception of theatricality.

The name of the theatre that opened on 31 October 1933 arose from Jarema's fascination with the circus. Cricot is an anagram of "to cyrk", reminding us of

Eric Satie's exclamation: "Let us not forget what we owe to the circus!" The lesson of Dada took the form, equally, of the example of Duchamp and of the rather later Kraków variety of Dada, one of the most fundamental genealogical layers of Kantor's mental formation.

Kantor's initial involvement with theatre was shaped by two sets of circumstances arising from the conditions in which artists operated, like conspirators, in the Underground Theatre. Kantor maintained, "Our idols were Mondrian, Malevich, and the Bauhaus," then immediately backtracked by saying that abstraction could not get the measure of the reality surrounding us, that "aesthetics is not the essence of art".

The first of the circumstances to shape Kantor's career was the cult of constructivism, introduced to Kantor by Pronaszko and nurtured by his susceptibility to everything new. The second set of circumstances was formed by the reality of the German occupation. "We told ourselves," Kantor said thirty-five years later at a press conference in Adelaide, "that abstraction was not adequate to the reality all around us . . . So we devised a concept of anti-art which, because of its basis in reality, could match up to the naked threat contained in the real world." Kantor's analysis concluded, "We annexed this threatening reality to the work of art."

This conceptual apparatus and the artistic choices it entailed bore fruit in the two premières of the Underground Theatre, which were a rallying-cry to young artists. The theatre was cut short by the grim night of Hitler's occupation of Poland, which scotched it at birth. The reception this apparatus received proved it was painters, above all, who were drawn to Kantor's theatre, and who were more than convinced of the need for tireless innovation. Their experience and practical mastery of the revolutionary Dada-futurist revolution on the one hand, and on the other, the part played in their creative radicalism by constructivism, prescribed certain tasks for them. *Balladyna*[3] and *The Return of Odysseus*[4] bore fruit in the form of certain decisions which marked Kantor's way forward. The discovery of the "reality of the lowest rank" and the annexation of this reality by the work of art had come about more or less through the common agency of Marcel Duchamp, who became Kantor's idol after the war, and Bruno Schulz, with his "degraded reality". As far as *theatre* was concerned, these were radically new developments. Endorsing the proposition about the "indivisibility" of the work of art proclaimed in his generation by Formism (developed in Kraków by the Pronaszko brothers as early as 1912), Kantor was maintaining after the Second World War that:

Theatre is the finest of the fine arts, because it resides between art and life.

In this fashion Kantor, the painter, was already showing another side of himself: the man of the theatre. The theatre, which incidentally had given him shelter during the socialist realist years when he worked as a scenographer, was thus responsible for his departure in October 1956 from the "professional" theatre forever. For Kantor, an artist who thought in "totalising" categories, it was quite unacceptable to relegate theatre to a position far in the rear of painting, which at the time was experiencing an avant-garde impetus that recalled the mood of the early twentieth century, abruptly throwing out one innovation after another. It was then that a decision was born to create a theatre which could keep pace with all these new discoveries in art. It had to be a painter's theatre.

The slogan, "Art forever in contact with reality," led Kantor to devise two basic provisos related to this proposition. The first was that the value systems of a work of art were always in conflict with this "reality." Secondly, the artist must always choose the side of life, and his departure from the domain of art – which is so strongly marked in the work of Duchamp – has to be seen as a continuous and unbroken process. "Total creativity is total reality" – is another way Kantor had of formulating this proposition, and it is recorded in many of the manifestos he devised in connection with particular productions.

His annihilation of the domain of art, and opposition to places of art sanctified by tradition, such as the museum or the stage, by no means implies a desertion, or rejection of them on the part of the artist. The artist tries to maintain his presence at all times, and takes special care that his personal decisions should not be merely "private". Undervaluing the prestige of art and the places that sanctify it, by no means indicates a desire to break with history or tradition. Kantor always kept his finger on the pulse of contemporary art; he was so fascinated by it that in Poland he had to endure the sneers of those who spoke of "gimmick merchants", always wanting to be "marginal" and keep their distance. Kantor strove to be a new guardian of the avant-garde "articles of faith". But to do this with conviction, he needed a rich cultural and historical context in which his discoveries could shine. It was this "marginal" vision of Kantor's that separated the avant-garde wheat from the pseudo-avant-garde chaff.

Saturated in this kind of thinking, Kantor's aesthetic stance permitted him to create his most outstanding theatrical work – *Dead Class* (1976) – at a moment of absolute crisis in the arts in the seventies. The Manifesto of the Theatre of Death which accompanied this dramatic event made very short work of pseudo-avant-garde phenomena, while breaking at the same time with the position Kantor had adopted in his Impossible Theatre.[5] Kantor had established in his own mind – in keeping with his understanding of the creative process – an idea of the "self-containedness" of his different creative stages and works of art. This led to his spectacular break with each previous period, which shocked artists who were so devoted to the idea of the "purity" of his art; he would even draw attention to the contradictions of his own position by some theoretical manifesto or poetic essay. The contradictions – it goes without saying – were located in a particular stage in the process, not in the process itself.

Kantor conceptualised the creative process as a kind of "monitoring" of the creative arts – his own, and those around him. This created the phenomenon we also find in contemporary poetry of the creative artist becoming at the same time the interpreter of his own work, and not just because he distrusts the critics, or feels contempt for what he considers to be their lack of sensitivity or incomprehension of his work. In Kantor's case, as the next chapter demonstrates, something more is at stake. His attack on the kind of professionalism that pigeon-holes art is combined with absolute hostility to dilettantism. An enormous respect for the craftsman, for the precise execution of every detail, are painterly attributes which illuminate Kantor's work with his actors and ensure the professionalism of the results. Kantor's actors, formed by the practice and theory of the Master, have no time for the counterfeits of so-called "experts". Three factors predominate: Kantor's actor is professionally "contaminated" by art, possessing wider artistic horizons than the average actor; he has the opportunity for persistent, step-by-step, deliberate work; and he benefits from the phenomenon of immediate identification with a role. Kantor has done away with verisimilitude, and the compromises it imposes. Hence his characteristic polemic with Edward Gordon Craig on the subject of the origins of the actor; hence, too, the troupe of wandering players carrying Kantor's artistic message around the world, like a sort of Big Top, or like Alexander Blok's modernist vision of the resurrection of a similar form of contact between the theatre and the audience.[6]

In Kantor's theatre, there is yet another feature operating against any simplistic propositions about the "impenetrability" or "elitism" of his work, propositions often offered maliciously, and aimed at devaluing his achievements. This is – to borrow a term from Kantor's great forerunner, Witkiewicz – his "insatiability". Kantor has an insatiable urge to encounter society, an urge he strove tirelessly to satisfy; and the response to this of an enormous public worldwide is sufficient evidence that not every revolutionary in art has to insult the audience. If, in the end, he is on the pro-art side in the Battle for Art, he can still be placed among the ranks of the innovators.

Notes

1 Cyprian Kamil Norwid (1823–1883) was the outstanding Polish poet of what in England might be called high Victorianism. He strongly resembles Gerard Manley Hopkins or Emily Dickinson in the way that he forces language against the grain of the conventional values of his time. He differs from them, however, in respect of his heterodox Messianism, generated in exile in Paris.

2 Andrzej Pronaszko (1888–1961, see Introduction, note 2) is one of the many unjustly neglected Polish twentieth century artists who worked in the more extreme "geometric" styles of the age.

3 *Balladyna* (1839), a play by the great Polish romantic poet Juliusz Słowacki, was directed by Kantor in 1942: "The first of six plays that were to present the history of Poland," noted one of the best Polish literary historians, Juliusz Krzyżanowski (*The History of Polish Literature*) Warsaw, PWN 1978.

4 *The Return of Odysseus* (1907) was the last of Stanisław Wyspiański's plays to be produced by Kantor in 1944, with a group of young artists who, like him, "disappeared" during the Nazi occupation. It was performed in the Underground Theatre, the name given to it by this underground group. Among the artists who took part was the eminent post-war painter Tadeusz Brzozowski; the creator of *Tygodnik Powszechny* – the only independent weekly to appear in Communist Poland – Jerzy Turowicz; and the respected critic, Mieczysław Porębski.

5 The period of Kantor's artistic activity (1972–1975) is discussed in the next chapter.

6 See Chapter 12, note 1, p. 109.

2

TOWARDS THE IMPOSSIBLE
THEATRE

(Conversation, June 1972)

KM: The organic relationship between your vision of the theatre and your attainments as a painter may lead us to the erroneous, but superficially plausible conclusion that Cricot 2 is for you a sort of domain of "painterly" experimentation transferred to the stage. Doubtless this is a simplification.

TK: And a very misleading one, however convenient it may be. In Cricot 2, I was forever giving concrete form to artistic ideas, and from time to time these coincided with the ideas of my paintings. But it was never a question of "transferring" painterly forms, or finding some plastic equivalent, or dashing off some contemporary picturesque style. Why do I depend upon the insights offered by painting? Not just because I'm a painter. Painting is the only art which has found the means to contradict itself, the only one which after the war, underwent a process of permanent revolution. Geometric abstractionism, *art informel*, neo-realism, "happenings", conceptual art, ephemeral art – these are just some of the stages in the evolution of painting. It keeps contradicting its own traditions and functions in ever-changing ways. The principal contemporary tendency, however, is to reject the representational function of the work of art, and to empty out the artificial depository which has been created for it. This depository has become a tame imitation of reality. The universal challenge thrown out to museums, galleries, the temples of art – all of this is actually just an implementation of the demands of the Dadas, and the postulates of that great revolutionary of art – Marcel Duchamp.

   If theatre renounces aesthetic-plastic values, it is forced to turn its attention away from the basic functions of the work of art, and theatre is, or should be, a work of art. In a word, painting has managed to save itself, thanks to its courage in going beyond the limited sphere of activities laid down for it by tradition.

KM: Does the theatre have the same chance of survival?

TK: Of course. Theatre must know how to profit from the inexhaustible radicalism of painting; but as I have already pointed out, this is by no means the same as saying that theatre has to become a pictorial art. Quite the contrary. It is generally recognised that the crisis in world theatre has come about as a consequence of rigid isolationism, of squeezing it into the tight corset of professional practices.

KM: Are you saying there is a need for the kind of theatre that could be called "total"?

TK: You could say something like that. At all events, every reform in the theatre has come about as a result of a broadly based appropriation of a totality of human thought, and its artistic re-working. There is no way you can separate the theatre of Meyerhold, Tairov, Piscator or Leon Schiller from the ideas of constructivism, futurism, Malevich's suprematism, Andrzej Pronaszko's version of constructivism,[1] the Dada movement, and so on.

KM: There are many people working in the theatre who share the view that the annexation of other artistic domains threatens the theatre.

TK: Of course. Thinking along these lines makes it impossible for the theatre to form its own *autonomous* structures – which has been the lot of other branches of art.

KM: How are we to understand a proposition about the "autonomous functions of the theatre"?

TK: The autonomous theatre I have in mind is a theatre which does not take the form of a reproducing apparatus, ie, a scientific interpretation of literature, but possesses its own independent reality.

KM: Do you think, then, that the crisis in contemporary theatre springs from its isolation?

TK: Not only. The crisis in contemporary theatre is above all the result of a lack of active, courageous commitment to the creative development of art, which throughout the twentieth century has found expression in a series of crucial discoveries. The theatre has simply ignored these, one after the other. It could not, for example, take on board the ideas of Duchamp, who unmasked the sacred taboo on the "space" reserved for the work of art. He revealed it to be an empty and squalid illusion, and reached out instead for a "real" reality. Theatre also seriously underrated the innovations of the surrealists, and the theory and practice of *art informel*,[2] which offered a radical new way of perceiving the work of art. And it even adopted the same attitude to the work of Craig,[3] which situated art within the domains of reality and fact which lay beyond the concepts of symbol and interpretation.

KM: I would like to ask what the relation is between your autonomous theatre and the notion of a totality of thought and action. "Autonomisation", so to speak, may conceal a danger of "narrow professionalism".

TK: This might have been the case if I had started thinking like the representatives of various avant-garde schools of thought I had occasion to meet in the West, for instance at the International Theatrical Workshop ITI in Dourdan, near Paris; people who are propounding an autonomous theatre in a purely professional context. They eliminate literary expression and replace it with the expressive devices of gesture and rudimentary sound. This is a particular way of quarrelling with the intellect; but it communicates only with people of very high intelligence.

KM: What does a literary text mean to you, in the theatrical context?

TK: Believing as I do that "replacing" the text, eliminating it by mechanical means, is a kind of intellectual sloppiness, I consider the literary text to be an important component containing an unparalleled degree of density and dynamism. It is a kind of a massive freight, which theatre can make good use of. "Real" theatre approaches the text as if it were a weighty, significant obstruction. My idea of an autonomous theatre highlights the apparent contradiction between my respect for the literary text and the autonomy of the spectacle – it is neither an explanation of the dramatic text, nor a translation of it into theatrical language, nor an interpretation or implementation of it. Nor is it, as I have said, the search for so-called "scenic equivalents", taking the form of a second, parallel "action", mistakenly called "autonomous". I give shape to this reality, to this tissue of contingencies, without bringing them into a logical, parallel, or contradictory relationship with the dramatic text; I establish fields of energy which sooner or later shatter the anecdotal shell of the drama.

KM: This is the view you advance in the manifesto of what you call Zero Theatre,[4] which goes against the idea of "development" in art and adopts, in the production of Witkiewicz's *The Madman and the Nun*,[5] a diametrically opposite direction – as you wrote, "Down below the normal order of things, by way of the slackening of bonds, by way of a loss of energy, a loss of expressiveness, a cooling of temperature, towards the void, to the zero region."

TK: In *The Madman and the Nun* the dramatic text was not performed, it was declaimed, commented on; the actors commented on it and then discarded it, returned to it and repeated it, never for a moment did they identify with the text.

KM: They improvised, in fact.

TK: That's just what they *didn't* do. The idea of separating text from action in order to "cleanse" it of its narratives became possible thanks to the annulment of incidents which were caught in a stage of weightlessness – a sort of juggling with them. This device had nothing to do with improvisation – a terribly traditional form of theatre that is occasional and makes use only of contingencies. In the Zero Theatre a much more dangerous element is at work – the element of chance.

KM: The next stage in the development of your autonomous theatre was the manifesto of the Theatre of Contingency[6] proclaimed at the time of *The Water Hen*.[7] The simple fact of removing the motivation from situations, events, contingent happenings, objects, and actions made them all existentially self-sufficient. This process threw into relief a radical change in the position and the "condition" of the actor.

TK: An actor *imitating* an action is always situated above the action. An actor *performing* an action in reality is placed on the same level as the action. In this fashion the basic hierarchy changes: object-actor, action-actor. An actor's performance must be the outcome of what I call his "preexistence", not weighed down, as yet, by the illusionism of the text. An actor does not develop his role, he does not create a character, he does not imitate his character, he is, above all, himself – an actor, with a whole fascinating panoply of tendencies and inclinations. He is not at all natural, he is altogether committed to his part, so that when he knows it properly he can discard it and blend it in with the scenic material which is always immediate, always free-flowing. This process of free activity must be profoundly human.

KM: In a word, then, the actor becomes the "ready-made" element in the realisation of a happening. How does the ensemble of actors look from this angle?

TK: I depend entirely upon the ensemble. The actor is a sort of pilgrim, like a member of a group of travelling players always looking for somewhere to drop anchor. Put on show, exposed to danger, he can only survive in his "group". The key moment occurs when the group gels and invisible bonds are formed between the actors, who manage to develop a sort of telepathic systematisation of individual elements. This telepathic linking affects the actor at a certain moment (and not at any other). Making an intuitive decision, the actor finds a voice and his role becomes imperative, before disappearing and giving way to another. Very detailed "pointing" of details, or interventions by the director, would be out of the question, and quite out of keeping with the basic principles of group work of this sort.

KM: Let's get back to the ITI Workshop in Dourdan, where six groups took part in Cricot 2, as well as in London's *La Mama*, Edinburgh's *Traverse Theatre*, *La Mama-Plexus* from New York, *The Theatre of Man* from Milan, *Théâtre Création* from Lausanne, and the *Pistolieteatern* from Stockholm.

TK: I took exception to the pseudo-avant-gardism of their artistic programme. Their performances can all be reduced to a single common denominator: a mechanical homogeneity of basic principles, slogans, terminology, problems and methods. Sheltering under the would-be humanistic banner of theatre as "the domain of basic human activity" by no means concealed the narrowly professional scope of their preoccupations, or the professionalism of their use of gesture and voice. I blame the "professionalism" of these young theatres on the fact that their conception of the workshop was contrived in isolation from the sphere of the new, vibrant European theatre, and other artistic disciplines. The idea of a drama festival of this sort is a good one; but it needs careful and deliberate planning to enable it to offer a platform to those artists whose inspiration is vital to the constant development of theatre.

KM: *The Shoemakers*, in Paris, was your second production of Witkacy abroad, after *The Country House*[8] in Baden-Baden (1966), and its subsequent performance in Yugoslavia by an international group (1969) at "i" (impossible) the convention of "happening" theatres. What do you think were your most significant experiences in the course of this work?

TK: My difficulties with the actors. Not because of the obscurity of

Witkacy's texts, purely technical difficulties. All my problems arose from the intrinsic characteristics of the French actor: he's a hireling, he's efficient, he's highly trained, but he's quite incapable of grasping those issues which the Polish amateur "wandering actor" can work through without difficulty if he keeps his mind on the job. The question of the actor's sensitivity – which is clearly highly relevant to the theatre I have created – has been aired once too often. The scenes that worked best were based on a kind of ornamental underpinning of the power of a monologic role. But the contact between the performers, and their intrinsic sense of humour, came out in the ensemble scenes. I had a different sort of problem on the first night. "The whole of Paris" ("*le tout Paris*") – that is, the dreadful Parisian glitterati – turned up in force.

Notes

1 Inevitably, Polish constructivism enjoyed a symbiotic relationship with the Russian version, although Pronaszko's was more lyrical.
2 Kantor's painting owes more to Matta and the French *informel* artists than to any other single source (except perhaps Duchamp).
3 Edward Gordon Craig (1872–1966), in particular his essay on the *Über-marionette*, had a huge influence in Central and Eastern Europe.
4 This concept may be compared to Roland Barthes' "zero degree of writing".
5 *The Madman and the Nun* is one of the most accessible and exportable of Witkacy's plays.
6 With this idea, Kantor began systematically deconstructing theatrical space.
7 The title of this play is hard to translate, since the Polish word for "hen" (*kurka*) suggests to Polish ears the word for "prostitute" (*kurwa*), a word which features in many everyday Polish objurgations.
8 This play by Witkacy, both in title and in content, is a challenge thrown at the feet of naturalism. *The Country House* (sometimes translated *The Little Manor*) is an allusion to Tadeusz Rittner's play *W Małym Domku (The Little House)*, acclaimed in Europe.

4. Tadeusz Kantor during an interview in June 1972. Photo: Jacek Bogucki

3

TADEUSZ KANTOR'S *CLOAKROOM*

(Film script, 1973–1974)

A documentary film by Krzysztof Miklaszewski
from the cycle entitled *The Anatomy of Performance*

Sequence One
Situation: the beginning of a performance. The crowd is thronging into the cloakroom, which has "iron" rails made of timber. The side entrance admits each visitor (spectator) separately, and they are then taken charge of by a pair of highly agitated Cloakroom Attendants.

The Cloakroom Attendants (Lesław and Wacław Janicki) get the queue organised; at the same time a voice comes out of a loud-hailer speaking in several different languages about the rights and the duties of the spectators.

THE CLOAKROOM ATTENDANTS:
– Please don't push. there's room for everybody.
– One moment, one moment!
– Form a neat queue, I can't see the end there, let's have nice straight rows everywhere please . . .
– Only employees of the theatre can come in without queuing.
– Let's keep to our queue, hang on there, you'll get your number . . .
– The cloakroom is obligatory, look, *you* weren't there, that chap was there.
– The cloakroom is open, ladies and gentlemen. We still have plenty of time.
– Next please.
– Not all at once, not all at once, there's a jam now.

– Hang on a bit . . .
– Please don't push, we've still got plenty of time, there will be room for everyone, room for everyone, room for everyone.
– If you please!
– The cloakroom, obligatory for everyone.
– Let's just move along, stop, and hand it over.
– Hold on, hold on, let's not block the way.
– The cloakroom's always right, the cloakroom's an absolute must.
– This is the place for our overcoats, our cases, our bags, our nylon macs, our umbrellas.

The Leader of the Mandelbaums (Zbigniew Gostomski) picks out individuals one at a time, hanging metal numbers round their necks and leading them to a particular sector of the auditorium.

THE LEADER OF THE MANDEL-BAUMS[1] (eager to sacrifice himself):
– Two Mandelbaums.
– Next please.
– Please keep your number for the inspector.

5. The stormy love story of the last female descendant of the line of the Abenceragi is acted out in a cloakroom, ruled over by the Cloakroom Attendants (the Janicki twins). Photo: Jacek Szmuc

THE CLOAKROOM ATTENDANTS:
– Next, please don't get into a muddle, there's room for everyone.
– The cloakroom's always right.
– If you will just allow me sir . . . fine, fine, it's been turned inside out, and quite worn under the arms, soaked in sweat, yes, the pile is coming out, it's fit for nothing, this one's been turned, too, and it smells stale. No, no.
– Shoes, shoes, shoes, look at this, look at this. He's got no socks on, got no socks on . . .
– Lets get them all hung up, leave them here, the cloakroom is only the beginning, only the beginning.
– The cloakroom's always right.
– Your coats are in our hands.
– And your fate too!
– Ha, ha . . .

When the Cloakroom Attendants have done their deeds, they laugh; their terrorist activities are backed up by orders barked from the loudhailers.

A VOICE:
– Depositing all your clothes in the cloakroom is the first and most important duty of the spectator.
– We are your only chance.
– Only loyalty to us guarantees you a real experience.

Sequence Two
Kantor speaks, sitting at a table at home. In the background there is an umbrella.

KANTOR:
– The current general opinion about my theatre is a sort of received wisdom that it is what you may call a painter's theatre, a sort of "plastic" theatre.
Obviously, this is an enormous misconception, which comes about simply as a consequence of misunderstanding the whole problem of contemporary theatre.

Sequence Three
Credits.

(On the soundtrack: laughter, a violin, shots.)

Sequence Four
Continuation of Kantor's statement.

KANTOR:
– The fact that I am a painter, and have a penchant for "the painterly",

is not a consequence of my seeing in painting certain visual-aesthetic values, even though Wyspiański[2] said that the theatre is fifty percent visual impressions, which is true. I wanted to say, and this is important, that I do not apply painterly methods in the theatre. Some people do. These people are decorative artists, really.

Sequence Five
Kantor, holding the script, standing with the actors on their level (the floor of the Krzysztofory), shows the Cloakroom Attendants what to do. The Janicki brothers repeat this after Kantor.

Kantor's voice is superimposed upon successive re-enactments.

KANTOR (interior monologue):
– The entrance to the theatre is through the cloakroom, the cloakroom is obligatory. Let's all get in the queue.
– If there is a cloakroom, then we'd better work out what this thing is for, its real function, but not put actors in it to strut about performing *Forefather's Eve*,[3] because that doesn't make sense.

Sequence Six
Jump to the finished performance. The same routine, perfected now. The Janicki gather the audience together.

THE CLOAKROOM ATTENDANTS:
– Keep to your places, please, don't get up.
– We are trying to maintain order and discipline.
– We accept no responsibility for property left in the cloakroom.
– The crowds are dwindling. Plenty of room for everyone; plenty of room for everyone.

Sequence Seven
A drawing showing the layout of the cloakroom in the production. After a moment, the camera shows that Kantor is holding the drawing in his hands seated at a long table full of sketches and notes. Kantor keeps nervously putting on and taking off his spectacles. He makes animated gestures interpreting his ideas.

KANTOR:
– If I give up on the artistic space – which is one way of talking about a *stage* – what have I got left? What I have left is precisely the auditorium. The auditorium has its own claim to fame; when you think about it, there's no such thing as an auditorium without a stage. And what is that really? This is one of the questions I am trying to pose in my "cloakroom" – I keep calling it that, because that's the title I would like to take the place of the play called *Lovelies and*

Dowdies.[4] This produces a random state, a state of gratuitousness. This gratuitous state, a theatre with no auditorium, no theatre, is a cloak-room, a waiting room, a theatre building, a store and a props room. The props room has a huge charm of its own. In the props room are all the pre-echoes of the reality which remains to be represented. In my effort to avoid presenting things, "producing" them, I store them. And the auditorium will be a store. I think of it partly as a store, partly as a wait-ing room, a bit like a cloakroom, and all of these things at once . . . every-thing at once, in my poor theatre.

Sequence Eight

People's reactions to the Cloakroom Attendants, who are resting like box-ers after a round in the ring, wiping each other with towels. A voice from a loudspeaker replaces their actions.

VOICE:

– Only complete trust in us ensures correct implementation of the desig-nated initiatives and selection proce-dures.

Rehearsal – the entrance of the Princess (Zofia Kalińska), while very strangely dressed actors crowd in from the backstage. The players shuf-fling along behind the Princess "play" suitors. One of them in a white uniform, the Captain of Lifeguards (Kazimierz Mikulski) keeps on shooting himself in the fore-head, and the Gypsy Violinist accom-panying him (Stanisław Rychlicki) plays a sentimental vocalise.

CLOAKROOM ATTENDANTS (res-training a group falling out of the door with the inscription "THEATRE" on it):

– One moment, one moment!

Kantor explains things to the actor with the skeleton representing the millionaire Sir Grant (Stanisław Gronkowski).

In the background, rehearsals, in the course of which Kantor shows the ensemble how to form the Procession of the Suitors paying court to their Beloved (interior monologue).

KANTOR (interior monologue):

– The gentleman first, then the lady . . . The gentleman may sit down for the time being.

– So these are actors, who represent no other reality existing outside themselves but exhibit themselves as themselves, and by doing so fulfil all the requirements of the sort of the-atre which I am involved with.

Sequence Nine
(The characters on show.)
Kantor backstage.

(As before.)

Kantor shows a sketch, and then there appears for comparison, one of the actors in a role from the play, in an actual situation from rehearsal or performance.

Rehearsal at the Krzysztofory: an actor (Bogdan Grzybowicz) runs into the acting space with a board on his shoulders. Kantor shows the actor how to hold his hands: the actor repeats the sequence and runs with the board to the exit.

Kantor comments from backstage.

Drawing – a sketch of a character come to life in a dramatic situation, when the actor playing Sir Grant (Wiesław Borowski), standing in a half-crouching position with wheels fixed to his legs, tries to turn them.

The man with the doors appears on the screen: the Cardinal.

Rehearsal in the Krzysztofory: Kantor explains to the actor with the doors (Jacek Stokłosa)

Kantor displays the drawing of the man with twice as many legs.

KANTOR:
– As an example, I could cite by name characters from *Lovelies and Dowdies.* These are people who have been formed in a special sort of way. For example, the man with the plank across his shoulders. This is a man who has some strange anatomical make-up, some sort of growth at the back of the torso, the presence of which he feels all the time. Inwardly too. He's a sort of curio.

KANTOR:
– That's how it should be. Bend your legs even less. Here you have to have them terribly tight, very contracted, really tight, otherwise you don't get the right effect. You have to be a bit frightened.

– The second of these people is a man with two wheels growing from his legs. He thinks he is a vehicle.

– Sometimes he dreams he's a ship's propellor, or that he's a vehicle.

– A man bearing doors, no one knows why, he just grew up with these doors, all he can do is open and shut them. Nothing else. Any representation of any state of mind is quite pointless in this context. All he can do is open and shut his doors.

KANTOR:
– You cannot split yourself from your doors.

– For instance, a man with two extra legs, who must be quite divided against himself, or have complexes, is alienated from the everyday world.

Rehearsal: the Cloakroom Attendants run in carrying the man with two pairs of legs sitting in an armchair, which overturns, and he can't cope with his strangely entangled pairs of legs. This is Pandeus (Zbigniew Bednarczyk).

The workshop: Kantor examines a drawing of the individual with two heads.

Rehearsal: scene with the man with two heads. This is Tarquinius (Jan Güntner) talking to Pandeus. The dialogue is punctuated by Tarquinius (also known as Quin) falling constantly flat on his face, and being propped up by the Cloakroom Attendants. Pandeus meanwhile keeps losing control over his four legs, with the Cook (Maria Stangret), also known as the Bestia Domestica, "ably assisting" him. She is the Attendants' Helper.

Kantor laughs.

Sequence Ten
Rehearsal: Kantor picks up a box from the floor, throws it, and stamps his foot.

Kantor goes up to two actresses, who have the crumpled box in their hands.

TARQUIN (Jan Güntner) to PANDEUS:
– This is just baseless catastrophism.

KANTOR:
– A man with two heads can happen . . . if there are animals with two heads – this could have a fatal effect on the possessor of the two heads in everyday life. Whereas in the theatre it provides the actors with exceptional opportunities . . .

PANDEUS:
– The most you can do is smoke. I have grown used to morphine. C_2H_5OH, alcoholism, is the hardest to treat, and anyway most drunkards don't want to stop drinking.

TARQUIN:
– Can I attain such proficiency without recognising in advance what danger I am in? Strength, strength must be solitary, it cannot be one with the person who employs it.

PANDEUS:
– Does not repression then give rise to the truest form of lust? All of this rushes to the brain and takes control of its hemispheres.

KANTOR:
– Right, you're fed up with that.

KANTOR (upset):
– We have to have everything we need for the rehearsal.

KANTOR:
– This is how you do it: first you look here, then you look there, then you look at him over here.

Kantor walking over to his table emphasises the point.

And this is phase two, phase two.

Then he swiftly returns to his discussion with the actors.

– These are the sorts of moments I am looking for: you are juveniles, but despite being juvenile, you are depraved – it's very difficult.

Sequence Eleven
The stage is prepared (for the performance). The two Juveniles, Nina and Liza, are talking to Tarquin, who is sitting in an armchair.

TARQUIN:
– I'm not in the least bit jealous of his past, I've already got over that, but you know if I found out about him doing something like that right now, something he shouldn't do . . . Believe me, my dear, I'd kill him like a dog.

The Juveniles are writhing about on the ground in erotic convulsions; they ruin the aforementioned box. The dialogue goes on in the middle of all this. One of the Cloakroom Attendants picks up Nina by the braces and dumps her on Pandeus's knee. He is droning on all the time, sizing up Nina from time to time. Tarquin goes round and round with his problem.

Nina is on Pandeus's knee.
Liza is writhing on the floor.

Kantor's interior monologue in this situation: he watches the scene and from time to time intervenes, with a gesture.

KANTOR (interior monologue):
– The production of *Lovelies and Dowdies* is an attempt at eliminating those immovable values that are seemingly obligatory for the theatre: performance, representation, the actors in action.

Sequence Twelve
Kantor at the rehearsal with his "score" in his hand. He is giving directions to the Cloakroom Attendants.

KANTOR (reading from his copy):
– Can we please have a bit more order, control, and sequence.

He suddenly shrieks at the Cloakroom Attendants:
– The sense of terror is growing!

Sequence Thirteen
Performance: the spectators are all

CLOAKROOM ATTENDANTS:
– From this side please.

seated. The Cloakroom Attendants patrol the whole extent of the Krzysztofory, in which the public is seated in facing rows, forming a corridor for the action leading from the cloakroom to the "entrance to the theatre".

The Cloakroom Attendants place sheets round the necks of the spectators in the front rows, like horse-collars.

Please hold your numbers up more, towards me. Please keep in order, and in sequence.

ONE OF THE SPECTATORS:
– And if I don't keep it, then what?

CLOAKROOM ATTENDANTS:
– To be safe and certain. (putting the sheets on the spectators)
The cloakroom's always right. Let's keep trying to keep things straight. Ah, how nice it is here, really splendid. Here, let's . . .

Sequence Fourteen
Kantor's workshop.

KANTOR:
– The problems taken on board by painting for the last 50 years, painting being the one 20th century art constantly exposed to the shocks of the avant-garde, meant that a "purely painterly" idea has enveloped the whole of art. It has quite simply embraced all the arts. I would like to cite here the words of Léger,[5] who was the first to formulate the idea that the art of our time must be unceasingly avant-garde. I am by no means sure that art was not *always* avant-garde: only in the past this concept did not exist.

Sequence Fifteen
Performance: The Cloakroom Attendants run around the auditorium with swathes of material, looking for fresh "victims". Kantor strolls around. The Cloakroom Attendants manage to corner one member of the audience and challenge him to repeat the sheet sequence. The commands making the victim sit and stand up are a refined form of obedience training. After some time the same fate befalls

THE CLOAKROOM ATTENDANTS:
– Up you get! Look sharp, look sharp, stand up! Come closer. First name, surname . . . come on, please . . . name, schooling, profession . . . I can't hear . . . please don't muddle things, please behave in an orderly fashion. Family in Poland? Abroad? Closer, stand back, next family please. He's handed it over or he's given it up . . . You can stand now. Next number, please.

another member of the audience. The remainder of the audience gloats over the "torture" inflicted on its neighbours.

Sequence Sixteen
Kantor with the actors at rehearsal. Kantor measures the space of the Krzysztofory – Kantor has interrupted the rehearsal because something isn't working out, and he sounds off all his complaints against the group.

Sequence Seventeen
Performance: after draping the audience with their covers, the Cloakroom Attendants run off, as if to put a distance between one another.

Sequence Eighteen
(Rehearsal intertwined with performance.)

Rehearsal: Kantor very worked up.

Performance: Cloakroom Attendants and the Leader of the Mandelbaums are drilling a section of the public.

Rehearsal: Kantor reads from the playscript.

Performance: The Cloakroom Attendants bully the candidates for the role of a Mandelbaum.

LOUDSPEAKER:
– Handing over your outer garments is the first and most important duty of the spectator.

KANTOR (raising his voice):
– We are in a theatre, and people don't sit in the cloakroom, they sit together in the auditorium.
(to Jan Güntner)
– No, excuse me, we are not going to make any *entré*. The atmosphere of this waiting room, of the whole inferno that has been created here, has to go deep inside you. And you have to play it like that. There's no room here for expression, because here, as I told you, what you have is terror. Art arouses that terror. And that's my latest manifesto: art as terror!

CLOAKROOM ATTENDANTS:
– And this is mine. Wait, wait.
– And this is mine.
– No. 42 isn't mine, please change it.
– We wait unceasingly.

KANTOR:
– Excuse me, but it seems to me as if the atmosphere had become very oppressive . . . and from this must spring . . . Witkiewicz.

CLOAKROOM ATTENDANTS:
– Close ranks, closer together, much more, come on now.

KANTOR:
– Crowd together, close ranks, close in.

CLOAKROOM ATTENDANTS (repeating Kantor's words after him as though remembering all the instructions from the rehearsal. They add):

- We must look more persistently in front of us, very persistently. More and more . . .

KANTOR (reading from a copy):
- As spectators who have paid for their tickets we have an inalienable right to sit down.
- Please. Getting up when signalled to do so signifies a transition to a state of active readiness.

Rehearsal: Kantor drills the Janicki brothers, comparing notes with the "score" all the time.

CLOAKROOM ATTENDANTS:
- Sit down, get up, stand up · · · pay attention, you're not allowed to change your seat . . . as a sign of the mounting tension of the production, we rush about more . . . up to the front, with tiny steps, virtually standing still. We draw back . . . move to the back of the stage, where the emotion is less intense. Now let's have a go. Crush together more, lightly bend the legs at the knees, legs bent . . . yes, crush together, crowd together, and now in the same place we retreat, crush, look fixedly to the front. . . .

Performance: Cloakroom Attendants repeat the text and gestures of the Leader of the Mandelbaums.

KANTOR (reading):
- Raise your shoulders, bend your arms at the elbows, incline them so as to take hold of your head.

Rehearsal in the empty Krzysztofory. Kantor continues to check what he has written. He gets worked up about it, shows it around, drills them himself.

THE LEADER OF THE MANDEL-
BAUMS and THE CLOAKROOM
ATTENDANTS:
- Shoulders in the air with an "inclination" to grab yourself by the head. Let's try . . .

Performance: Cloakroom Attendants and the Leader of the Mandelbaums – checking that the audience are paying proper attention, rebuking them, pulling faces and casting furtive glances at them.

KANTOR:
- Now we come to the textual and semantic sphere.

Rehearsal: Kantor.

THE LEADER OF THE MANDEL-
BAUMS and THE CLOAKROOM
ATTENDANTS:
- Thrust together, insulted, insistently, categorically, and viciously, hope-

Performance: the whole of the auditorium fails to participate in the drill, struck by the absurdity of the situation. The Cloakroom Attendants escalate the action all the while. The ones who've been drilled are weaker and weaker, therefore more and more ridiculous.

Rehearsal: Kantor (shows his increasingly intense feelings with a wave of his hand).

Performance: the group of the spectators who have been drilled in the parts of Mandelbaums, gathered in the cloakroom offstage, are dressing. The audience slip on black Jewish gaberdines, put on beards, add hats on top – in short, they turn into Mandelbaums.

Sequence Nineteen
The workshop: Kantor behind the table.

Sequence Twenty
Rehearsal: Kantor to the ensemble crowding round the "Entrance to the Theatre".

less . . . mixture of feelings, viciousness, pressure, frenzy, fury, and now heavy breathing too . . . yes, yes, more and more, still more . . . in the climactic moments of heavy breathing they walk into the rumble of gunfire. This expresses all their feelings at once.

KANTOR:
– We have to make this range from the amiable to the vicious.

VOICES:
– Marek . . . Marek . . . give me . . .
– Please put on your coat and hat and . . . a number.
– Please fasten it properly under the chin, with the number on top.

KANTOR:
– Acting is a surrogate activity. It stands in for all passions, ardours, struggles, the conflicts of life, only in a pure state, ie, it cleanses them from the grime of life.

KANTOR:
– I have changed this scene a little. The suitors come in and with the help of the Cloakroom Attendants they start to drive the children into the hen-coop. Suitors, yes suitors. And then Cloakroom Attendants. They will throw the Mandelbaums out of the door. They will throw them out like a rag doll. One Mandelbaum is very striking, then two, three, and when there are as many as ten, the hall is already full, and with fifteen, twenty, we can actually finish the performance . . .

Sequence Twenty-one
Rehearsal: The Cloakroom Attendants, together with the Cook, drive the Princess into the cage. They are accompanied by the Cook and the train of Suitors. Kantor hovers round all the time, urging them on with gestures.

KANTOR: to the Cloakroom Attendants.

– You are driving her to her death.

Sequence Twenty-two
Rehearsal: Kantor interrupts a scene.

KANTOR:
– From now to the very end Zofia is the star attraction for this whole bunch of . . . metaphysicians.

Sequence Twenty-three
Driving the "hen" (Princess, played by Zofia Kalińska) into the hen-coop cage.

Performance: Zofia looks out of the cage.

ZOFIA:
– I will comfort you.

Rehearsal: Tarquin, or the Man with Two Heads (Jan Güntner) tries to go into the cage after Zofia. Kantor, together with the whole group, follows these efforts.

KANTOR (to Güntner):
– So do it like this: . . .
Open it, she's waiting, and that's dangerous, while she's waiting, you can get a good look, see what she's got here, her . . . sex.

Performance: Re-run of this situation "in fair copy".

Rehearsal: Kantor to the actors.

KANTOR:
– Louder, shout with more force.

Performance: the Suitors listen to the dialogue of Tarquin and Zofia, as do the spectators, driven from their seats by the Cloakroom Attendants.

TARQUIN (to Zofia):
– How disgusting this is, I really hate you.

CLOAKROOM ATTENDANTS (hurrying the spectators along):
– Back to your places please.

Rehearsal: Kantor still very preoccupied by Güntner.

KANTOR (to Güntner):
– Jan, old chap, can you just arrange your head to allow this lady to hide it, then she'll grab – with her hands – that other head . . .

Sequence Twenty-four
Performance: Cloakroom Attendants above the cage, in which Tarquin, already driven in, is next to Zofia. Sir Grant (the Man with the Skeleton), played by Stanisław Gronkowski, drops in.

SIR GRANT:
– Zofia my love, Zofia my dear, I confess it all, I gave you a pill, you once promised me . . . it's already beginning to work, alas prematurely . . . It's supposed to start after four hours at the earliest . . . I bless you, my dear, you promised, we can give it a try anyway.

Sequence Twenty-five
The workshop: Kantor at the table with the sketches for *Lovelies and Dowdies*

KANTOR:
– An artist who says he has his own feelings is lying. He is dependent on a whole range of factors which lie beyond him. Perhaps it's true he doesn't actually realise this. Obviously, he is free to decide that it's his business entirely. But I still think that is fraudulent. On the other hand, I count it honest if I lay bare the whole way that art depends upon reality, upon what's going on all around us. And that is why in Poland they think I am under certain influences, because I talk too much about this environment which surrounds me. Because you have to realise that artists talk only about themselves, and talk in such a way as to suggest that they dreamed up everything: which is untrue . . .

Sequence Twenty-six
Performance: Cloakroom Attendants turn over the cage/hen-house with Zofia and Tarquin in it. The cage is covered with a cloth. Amorous talk comes from the cage, punctuated by the nasty comments of the Cloakroom Attendants.

VOICE OF ZOFIA:
– My darling, but you must truly be mine. If not, you will choke on my poison, just as others have. I am yours, yours.

VOICE OF TARQUIN:
– No, no, I want only your soul.

CLOAKROOM ATTENDANTS:
– Go on, get stuck in.

VOICE OF ZOFIA:
– I feel that, I feel it.

Sequence Twenty-seven
The Cloakroom Attendants open and close the door. Through the half-open door you can hear the splash of water and see people dancing under the "shower" and washing before supper. Interior monologue of Kantor, watching this scene.

KANTOR (interior monologue):
– And it's odd, that in our theatrical milieu no-one seems to think that the theatre has to develop. They talk about performances, brilliant directors, magnificent productions. But no-one talks about development.

Sequence Twenty-eight
(Single combat.)
Rehearsal: Kantor measures the Cook's trap-machine, which is intended to annihilate Tarquin.

KANTOR to the COOK (Maria Stangret):
– This sort of movement, measuring it, check that it will work . . . this . . . have a go . . . see if you can go like that.

Performance: The Cook goes off with the trolley. Tarquin is ready to struggle with the Cloakroom Attendants; he shouts.

Rehearsal: The Cloakroom Attendants (the Janicki brothers) try out the trap many times over, they practice positions for the "Japanese Duel".

TARQUIN:
– I'll shoot you like a mad dog and then myself, him, I'll kill them all.

Performance: Tarquin caught, crammed into the trap, is wheeled off by the Cook (who was impersonating the Princess).
People's different reactions.

KANTOR (showing the sequences of the duel to the Janicki twins):
– Stop! En garde, retreat.

Sequence Twenty-nine
Devouring the Princess. The Mandelbaums attack the cage with Zofia in it. Zofia vanishes, apparently torn to pieces by the mob. The Mandelbaums perform a burial service over the empty cage.

KANTOR (interior monologue):
– As far as I was concerned, the most important thing in this production was to disclose the multiplicity of all the elements I had selected, so that the spectators, because they are what count all the while, felt the impossibility (which is crucial) of taking in the whole of the performance from a spectator's standpoint.

Sequence Thirty
The Cook pulls the Princess's skin triumphantly out of the cage, the Cloakroom Attendants drop in from the Cloakroom, this time they are trying to throw the general public out of the Cloakroom. Thus the situation returns to where it started from, with the access through the cloakroom: only in reverse.

CLOAKROOM ATTENDANTS:
– Closing time, please stand in a queue with your numbers, please get ready. Even numbers stand first. We're closing the cloakroom shortly.

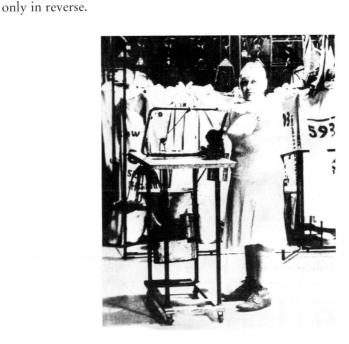

6. Half-witted Cook, dubbed the "Bestia Domestica" with wonderful kitchen trolley in *Lovelies and Dowdies*. Photo: Jacek Szmuć

Notes

1 The Mandelbaums are (as the name suggests) Jewish, and have a sort of grotesque "rabbinical" role which in another context might seem anti-Semitic (cf. the exterminated rabbi who sings cabaret songs – played by Kantor's wife, Maria Stangret – in *Wielopole*).

2 Stanisław Wyspiański (1869–1907) is the first great modernist playwright in Polish, and his dramatisations of fundamental Polish national anxieties, especially in *The Wedding* (1901) and *Liberation* (1903), suggest Yeats and Synge. He was also a fine, if derivative, painter and decorative artist.

3 The benchmark of Polish romantic art is Adam Mickiewicz's hugely eccentric and massively influential closet epic drama *Dziady* (Forefather's Eve) (1823–33). Kantor's piece is a satirical interpretation of one of the most fascinating performances in Polish theatrical history of this play directed by Konrad Swinarski in 1973. The director, who died tragically early (1975) also ensconced his actors in a cloakroom.

4 Also known as *Dainty Shapes and Hairy Apes*.

5 Ferdinand Léger (1881–1955) appealed to Kantor by virtue of an integration of organic and inorganic forms analogous to Kantor's own.

LOVELIES AND DOWDIES

(Critical Commentary, 1974)

Witkiewicz's *Lovelies and Dowdies,* in Kantor's staging, represents his attempt at an Impossible Theatre. Kantor, stripping Witkiewicz's text of its literary "finish", manages in consequence to free it of imitative routines. Each character springs to life and takes shape under the very eyes of the spectator, who is dragged into the action of the play. Reduced in this fashion to the dimensions of mere existence, the protagonists are fatally compromised. The "stormy love story of the last female descendant of the line of the Abenceragi" is acted out in a theatre cloakroom, ruled over by two identical twins (like two mutant clones), the male and female Cloakroom Attendants (Lesław and Wacław Janicki).[1] They are assisted in their "campaign of repression" by a half-witted Cook, dubbed the "Bestia Domestica" (Kantor's wife, Maria Stangret),[2] who devotes herself to cleaning the weird and wonderful kitchen trolley as if to a task of the utmost significance. The trolley has clamped shut like a trap on one of the principal protagonists, Tarquin (Bogdan Grzybowicz). The Cloakroom Attendants not only terrorise the audience, controlling in some measure the degree of their participation in the performance, they also direct the way the actors perform: summoned and allowed in, they are then dismissed, thrown out of the hessian door bearing the magic inscription "Entrance to the Theatre".[3] Each of the characters, reduced to this grotesque dimension of existence, is restricted to a single set of complex behavioural factors. So Princess Zofia (Zofia Kalińska) – Witkacy's lascivious and stylish vamp, who searches for release in her amorous excesses and drug sessions – is for Kantor just an old frump, a real "henpecker" who is driven into a genuine chicken coop, which is crushed to pieces in the end by the mob of forty Mandelbaums.[4] This mob of "faceless and disengaged" masculinity is played by ordinary – and quite unprepared – members of the audience, selected just before they went into the theatre. The Leader of the Mandelbaums (Zbigniew Gostomski), like the leader of a chorus, directs their performance from a loudspeaker, referring to an admonitory text, "Rules for the Audience".

Zofia, a blowsy, sensual blonde, and the portrayal, mental and physical, of her doleful suitors – the aforementioned Tarquin, with two heads growing from his torso like the Jack in a pack of cards, and Pandeus (Zbigniew Bednarczyk), who has been given an extra pair of legs – comprise a wretched tragedy of no less wretched characters, acted out by a troupe of actors even more wretched in their carnival guise.

7. Witkiewicz's *Lovelies and Dowdies*, in Tadeusz Kantor's staging, represents his attempt at an Impossible Theatre. Photo: Jacek Szmuc

The outcome is that the "real existence" of particular individuals, subjected to these principles of deformation, is so powerful that there is no longer any room left for psychologising. When the Cloakroom Attendants let them get a word in edgeways, the actors speak the text just as much among themselves as to the audience – a familiar signal that contact is being made. This breaks the "bond" established the moment before, and they plunge back into the peculiar ritualistic preoccupations of their everyday lives. This is how it is with the Cook's frantic cleaning of the trap, the Cardinal's obsessive opening of the door, and Sir Grant's futile sand-scattering. Kantor has created every character in this "poor realm" of Princess Zofia with a well-defined obsession, which motivates events on the one hand and annihilates them on

8. The Cloakroom Attendants terrorise the whole auditorium, controlling in some measure the degree of their participation in the performance. The audience is ridiculed, blackmailed and interrogated. Photo: Jacek Szmuc

the other. For instance: Witkacy's proud Cardinal, Dr Nino de Gewacz (Krzysztof Miklaszewski),[5] is in Kantor's version a beggarly parish priest, who has grown a lift on his back – the real thing, made of wood and iron, with heavy doors. The Tsarist Captain (Kazimierz Mikulski) spends his time endlessly committing suicide to the accompaniment of music which pierces his Slav soul, played by a barefoot Gypsy Street Musician (Jacek Stokłosa). The English lord known as Sir Grant (Wojciech Łodyński), humping a skeleton on his back and then eagerly burying it and digging it up again out of a heap of dirty sand, and the American Millionaire (Stanisław Rychlicki), whose dreams of spiritual flight materialise in the shape of two shabby bicycle wheels screwed to his feet, carrying on a drawing room discussion about the effects and the harmfulness of drugs. The two Hysterical Teenagers (Mirosława Rychlicka and Hanna Szymańska) keep indulging over and over again in their first Act of Masturbation, and look as if they (like Tarquin) have been initiated into the highest mysteries.

This, then, is the train of Suitors which make up the Kantor panoptic. Its complex of inner drives is more or less what Witkacy must have dreamed of when he invented his theory of interdirectional stresses.[6] Another monstrous personage crowns the parade – a Hermaphrodite with a Plank (Maria Górecka), darting like a startled rat from one end of the cloakroom to the other.

Colette Godard, highly respected reviewer from the influential French daily *Le Monde* (19 and 20 April 1974) described the mood of a Kantor production in the following terms:

It has the spirit of a wondrous tale, an unsettling absurd game. It comes into being all mixed up with characters who are like dead rag dolls, who shout, dance with skeletons in their arms, run restlessly about, give themselves up with feverish detachment to a range of activities. We don't know if they are talking to themselves or addressing us. They create an organised disorder, and invite us with a magnanimous sense of hospitality to witness the birth and growth of their own personal reality (. . .) It has its being in the midst of a nightmare, born of a terrifying existence, but which fortifies us so long as it is just a dream, and not life. And that is exactly what the theatre of Witkiewicz is like. It is not the theatre of the absurd: it is absurdity itself, made utterly new, and with such audacity, such vitality, that it draws us into a whirlpool of invigorating fresh air. This is a paradox; but it is a fact.

Notes

1 The twin Janicki brothers were a godsend to Kantor. Not only did they look intrinsically comical, they gave superb performances in "twin" roles and seemed to become a walking metaphor for his special quarrel with "representation". See Afterword.

2 Kantor enjoyed casting his wife (a known painter), in these degrading roles: thereby paying her a compliment, as a key figure in a degraded reality.

3 Which, of course, it is not, in any normal sense.

4 This was a comic scene played by the Cloakroom Attendants who attempt to shoo the Princess into a cage much as one would shoo a hen into a coop.

5 The author (Krzysztof Miklaszewski) was crucial to Kantor's work. He may not have had the biggest parts, but he had an exceptional overview of what was going on, and after Kantor's death was perhaps the only actor to offer to tell the public at large about the methods Kantor employed to elicit extraordinary performances from his "family".

6 Very little of Witkacy's voluminous, offbeat theoretical writing about art and literature has been translated into English. His absurdisms, as with Kantor, went hand in hand with an obsessive formalism.

9. Sir Grant (the Man with the Skeleton) in a love dialogue with Princess Zofia ("hen" in a coop) in *Lovelies and Dowdies*. Photo: Jacek Szmuc

5

DEAD CLASS, OR A NEW TREATISE ON MANNEQUINS

(Conversation, October 1975)

KM: The idea you are currently working on with the Cricot 2 ensemble has been given the generic subtitle of a "dramatic séance",[1] and you have made Witkiewicz one of the participants. Does the "space" you have set aside for Witkiewicz equate with any specific function in your text as it takes shape?

TK: Most definitely. I haven't yet worked out a way of getting it into the poster that this is also a play by Witkiewicz, because his play, *Tumour Brainard*[2] scarcely exists in my production. Now you see it, now you don't: it is not my intention that my production should be a production of Witkacy's play. There *are* certain personages, certain well-defined situations, but only to bring out the tension between theatrical reality and some other factitious reality. That is the role of the "pre-existing" text, the text that existed before the performance, the literary text, in this case, the text of a play.

KM: Are the characters given Witkacian names?

TK: As in the case of former Cricot productions, Witkacy's characters are overlaid by the characters of the actual performance. On the school benches in *Dead Class* sit the Prostitute-Lunatic, the Woman with a Mechanical Cradle, the Woman Behind the Window, the Old Man with a Bicycle, the Old Man from the Lavatory, the Old Man Pederast, the Paralytics, and the Repeat-a-year Hourglass Bearer. The Beadle from the Good Old Days and Charlady-Death keep up their good work as spiritual guardians of these "eternal pupils". All the characters make use from time to time of Witkacy's text: for instance, the Old Man from the Lavatory is Tumour Brainard, the Woman with the Mechanical Cradle is Rozhulantyna, and so on.

KM: So the matrix derived from the Witkacy characters is supplemented by two other characters: the Beadle and the Charlady ...

TK: It's worth pausing for a moment on the Charlady. She represents the *Putzfrau* – the type of person who cleans school buildings – and she is weighed down with all the tools of her trade: brooms and brushes big and little, shovels and buckets. In particular, she has a huge brush that takes the place of a scythe. A completely expressionless face; movements which are set, precise, mechanical, and repeated hundreds of times. She starts by tidying up things, but soon turns her

10. School pranks in *Dead Class*, with the Old Man with the Bicycle (Andrzej Wełmiński) and the Lady Behind the Window (Zbigniew Gostomski). Photo: Jacek Barcz

attention to people as well. A ritual aspect dominates her activities: washing the actors' bodies puts us in mind of the last rites for the dead. This is all the more intelligible as her activities become more and more comprehensive, and she begins to be identified with death. In this way, the collection of old people turns into the *Dead Class*.

KM: Another figure you summon to your "séance" is Bruno Schulz.[3] This is especially interesting in view of the fact that the name of the famous author of *The Sanatorium under the Sign of the Hourglass* appears here for the first time in your work.

TK: Our entire generation grew up in the shadow of Schulz, and then many of us forgot about him, or only half remembered him. Then the sixties rediscovered Schulz's prose, but only in the context of their own investigations. Kinship with Schulz, or indeed the continuation of a Schulzian tradition, only became reality for us in the seventies. When

I wanted to grasp the idea of a "degraded reality" – a category created in Polish culture by Schulz, among others – I had first to make my pilgrimage from *art informel* to the *Emballages Manifesto*.[4]

KM: I was particularly fascinated by the routine you use to begin your "séance". As members of the audience enter the theatre, they are confronted by school benches with people sitting on them, and their dead gestures express an urge to break away from the other members of the group. One hand is timidly raised, then another, and a third, and soon they are all rivalling one another for attention. In the end, a monumental pyramid of hands and torsos towers majestically over the auditorium. This is a sort of "game with the void".

TK: To be more precise, it is a development of my Zero Theatre.[5] That "void" is the basis of my concern with the "unseen". It all forms part of the problematic, as I emphasised in 1963, connected with the orientation "downwards", an orientation which has a chance of approximating to reality.

KM: Schulz, shaping and disclosing all around himself a "degraded reality", wrote: "If it were only possible . . . to discover, at the end of some long and winding road, a second childhood, and to have it all over again in its boundless plenitude – that would be the beginning of 'the age of genius'.[6] My ideal is to attain childhood. That really would be attaining true maturity." Your return to the reality of childhood has much of the Schulzean spirit in it.

TK: That kind of thing, yes, although my work is proceeding in a slightly different direction towards "degraded reality". I was drawn to this by my experiences of the sixties: which is to say, by a series of insights related to an understanding of death. Allow me to translate those experiences into an image I can present to you in terms of my theatrical "séance". In come some human beings in the twilight of their lives, dressed in rustic mourning clothes, who have become "ingrown" with the corpses of children. These child-corpses, growing in some kind of an extra-biological dimension, are like parasitic excrescences on their bodies. They are actually the same person in a larval form which contains the entire memory of their childhood, discarded and forgotten out of insensitivity because of the mindless drudgery of everyday life, which strips us of the capacity to grasp the bigger picture. It is the facticity of everyday life which kills our ability to imagine the past. This is the basis for all my thinking on this subject. This is consistent with what I said in my *Anti-exhibition* of 1963. In my "séance" I try to demonstrate how our past becomes a forgotten element, where feelings, photographic images, and likenesses we once felt close to lie scattered, together with clothes, faces, accidental things. Their "dead" state, however, is deceptive, as it only takes a slight shift for them to begin living in memory and interacting with the present. Images like these are not the by-product of boredom or middle-aged sentimentality; they bear witness to the urge to discover a full, rich life, the life of the past, present, and future.

KM: In a famous letter to Witkiewicz, Schulz defined the "degraded reality" captured in *Cinnamon Shops* in the following way: "The substance of the reality of those times is in a state of constant ferment, putting forth new shoots, living with a life of its own. There is no such thing as a dead object, a hard-edged object, an object with strict limits. Everything flows beyond its boundaries, as if trying to break free of them at the earliest opportunity."

TK: Schulz's vision impregnated the thinking of my entire generation. But we must remember that this is 1975, and therefore we absolutely must add something of our own to that vision. This "destructive", "scandalous", anti-constructive trend must lead us towards an understanding of death: and in this context death makes an appearance in the guise of the object-without-an-image, or "l'objet trouvé".

KM: In the work you have been doing over the last ten years, you have devised and animated many ideas aimed at destroying the self-sufficiency of the work of art. The happening-style "readymade reality"; the appropriation of life and reality by a series of rituals, artistic interventions and decisions; all those instances of "decollage" of living reality in your Cricot 2 productions, underlined the urgent need to go on developing the art of the theatre.

TK: Like everything fascinating, this too degenerated into a convention practised all over the place, senseless and vulgar. But these quasi-ritualistic manipulations of reality, bound up with my challenge to the status of art and of the "space" (as carried out in *Lovelies and Dowdies*)[7] reserved for art, gradually acquired a different point, a different significance.

KM: Are you thinking about your latest experiments with Cricot 2?

TK: Yes. In *Lovelies and Dowdies* the convention I had adopted in *The Water Hen* was still in evidence – the incredible importance of the physical presence of the object. Everything had to be concretely acted out there and then, by which I mean *among* those spectators in the Krzysztofory. By analogy, the artistically represented object (for example my *Chair* project in Oslo),[8] stripped of its expressiveness, its interrelations, its "attitude", its significance in some communicative scheme, and its "message", was turned into a non-entity, a sort of mock-up for the stage. The enigmatic sequences in the "Impossible Theatre" were examples of something different in kind: actions and situations were enclosed within their own sphere of reference, losing contact with their environment. In the manifesto I called *Cambriollage*,[9] I shifted the terms of reference altogether, illicitly, into a terrain where tangible reality was extended into its "unseen projection". Face to face with experiments of this kind, such categories as thought, memory, and time acquire a new kind of significance.

KM: Time after time you have emphasised that to think in terms of theatre is to think in terms of the plastic arts. If this is so, it leaves me curious as to where you stand in relation to questions of language and the conceptual dimension.

TK: You are touching upon one of the most important elements of my undertaking. This is the certainty, which I affirm with ever-increasing conviction, that to grasp the meaning of life in a work of art, you must pass by the way in which there is no life. This process of "dematerialisation" has been a constant factor along my theatrical way, even when the linguistic and conceptual element has remained marginal.

KM: Nowadays, when such ideas have become commonplace, generally accepted, and fashionable, you have to be on your guard against them.

TK: There certainly is quite a crowd of followers for at least a part of all this, and there are people today who have adopted as their slogan the Dada phrase "Total Art", or "Everything is art, everybody is an artist, art is in the mind", etc. I cannot stand crowds. I wrote a draft of my new manifesto as long ago as 1973, and I make reference in it to this unnatural state of affairs. It begins like this: "Ever since the Battle of Verdun, the Cabaret Voltaire, and Marcel Duchamp's *Water-Closet*, when the artistic status quo was drowned out by the roar of Big Bertha, the 'decisive intervention' became the one remaining chance of drawing attention to some new thing that had not yet entered consciousness, and which might inspire a work of art, might give art a direction. But in recent times, thousands of mediocrities perpetrate these 'interventions' without let or hindrance. We have lived to witness a process of remorseless banality and conventionality in the area of creativity."

KM: The corpses of children which the Old Folk hoist on to their shoulders when they go back to their schoolroom are mannequins. Another mannequin doubles for the Beadle. Evidently, the use of mannequins is not a matter of chance, as far as your productions are concerned.

TK: No, you're right, although the mannequin initially played an incidental part. I have always been convinced that any new period of creativity must start with factors which are relatively insignificant and scarcely perceptible, having little in common with the course of action I had previously been engaged upon. The mannequins in my production of *The Water Hen* (1976), and in *The Shoemakers* (1970), had specific parts to play: they took the form of metaphysical extensions – as if the actors had an additional organ which was somehow his master. The mannequins used on a large scale in my production of Słowacki's *Balladyna*[10] were doubled by living figures. They seemed to be endowed with a higher awareness, by virtue of the "completeness" of their existence. They had already been clearly stamped with the imprint of death.

KM: At this point we should invoke the *Treatise on Mannequins* by Schulz.

TK: If I am paying conscious homage to Schulz, then it is certainly in this third phase. Following *The Eternal Wanderer* and *Wrapped People*, the mannequin I made use of in 1967 in the Cricot Theatre was a constant presence which appeared in my *Collections*, in keeping with my conviction that only reality of the lowest rank, the poorest things, stripped of all glamour, are fit to demonstrate the whole of their facticity in a work of art. Mannequins also have their no-go area.

KM: And this is bound up with their origins and evolution?

TK: Yes. The existence of these creatures, who have been made in man's image, but "godlessly", by illicit methods, is the outcome of a heretical set of operations, a manifestation of some Dark, Nocturnal, Turbulent aspect of human enterprise. Crime and the Mark of Death as the sources of knowledge. And this is where I come to my own ideas.

KM: What we might call the *New Treatise on Mannequins*.

TK: I have a vague and inexplicable sense that by the agency of that humanoid, which is like the living reality but devoid of consciousness or purpose, the terrible remittance of Death and Nothingness comes down to us, becoming the grounds – at the same time – for transgression, repudiation, and attraction, indictment and fascination. The appearance of the mannequin coincides with my most powerful conviction that life can be expressed in art only by the absence of life, by an appeal to death. What in Schulz was only a premonition can find its material embodiment in me, someone better endowed with the consciousness of our age, the age that killed Schulz. And the most important thing of all: the mannequin in my theatre is designed to serve as a model through which the powerful sensation of death, and the lot of the dead, may be experienced. A model for the living actor.

KM: In 1907, Edward Gordon Craig wrote: "I call with all the strength I command for the return of this idea – of the Übermarionette – to the theatre: and when it returns once more, and people see it, it will, for sure, command such a quantity of love that people will be able to make

11. Miklaszewski as the Beadle in *Dead Class*, with his mannequin, and Kantor.
Photo: Jacek Barcz

merry according to the ancient ceremonies, they will again bow to the Creative Principle and feel the joy of life, and to Death they will pay godly, joyful homage."[11]

TK: I do not believe the mannequin could ever take the place of the living actor, as Craig wished, and Kleist too. To demonstrate this I need only observe the image, the image suggestively described by Craig, of the actor making his first appearance, which contradicts any notion that the marionette has usurped the place of the actor in the theatre. In my view, the moment the actor appears for the first time in front of the audience was – to use present-day terminology – revolutionary and avant-garde. In my manifesto of the Theatre of Death, which accompanies the séance-like *Dead Class*, I try to give an accurate account of this image, in which the course of events runs directly counter to Craig's argument. The decision to break with the cult of the collective, the act of severance (*rupture*) cannot be interpreted by reference to a taste for the exotic, the thirst for fame, or the hidden inclinations of the actor.

In my Theatre of Death I give the following description of this fascinating state of affairs:

> Face to face with those who have remained on the "other side", is the man who pretends to be the same as they are: but in spite of that (and because of some secret and brilliant function) he is forever remote, terrifyingly "other" like a dead man cut off by some invisible barrier – no less frightening or incommunicable because its true significance and menace are only made manifest in dreams. It is as though some dazzling, tragically carnivalesque image of man has suddenly been glimpsed in a blinding flash of light, which those on the other side have seen for the first time, as though seeing, in fact, themselves. This is, you might say, a metaphysical shock. This living vision of man looming out of the mists, seeming to press tirelessly on, is bitter evidence of his new human condition – just human; of his responsibilities and his tragic consciousness, measuring his fate by a scale of values that is implacable and absolute, the scale of death.

This is what I am talking about, this is what I base my performances on. This moment of shock I refer to has become trivialised at the end of a tradition lasting thousands of years; it is threadbare and meaningless in our time. Even though it might be over-ambitious, my concern is to re-validate that moment of shock as it was in the beginning. Thanks to the functions recollected in the parable constructed between the actor and the audience (based on Craig's vision), a distance is established comparable to the distance between the living and the dead. If a man falls over and dies in the street, a barrier is set up between him and the observer which the observer senses for the first time; he then "sees" this man for the first time. This man is the actor, deceptively like us, yet at the same time irremediably "other", the other side of an impassable barrier.

The most important course of action is the victory of art and the shaping of this art – a virtually impossible task, but utopia is always fascinating – to an unimagineable degree of expressiveness.

12. The Theatre of Automata (finale of *Dead Class*). Photo: Jacek Barcz

KM: It seems to me that the power of the séance over the spectator will become increasingly greater, and more easily verified, as we draw closer to the moment when our knowledge of death becomes more conscious, in the way it was in Romantic and Baroque art; and as it still is in the culture of the Middle East and the Far East, and in American and Latin-American art.

Notes

1   The Polish word connotes "session" as well as "performance" and (as in spiritualism) "séance".

2   S I Witkiewicz, *Tumor Mózgowicz* (1920).

3   Bruno Schulz (1892–1942) is by common consent one of the most impressive talents in Polish modernism. His short stories have been extremely well translated by Celina Wieniawska.

4   The formlessness of *informel* art is more apparent than real: the point about it (and the *emballages*) is that they both suggest shapes and patterns which have come into being by chance but redefine the spaces they occupy.

5   In the early sixties Kantor was particularly preoccupied by different kinds of minimalism and conceptualism (cf p. 159) Umbrellas, for example, as *objets trouvés* became an obsessive motif, signifying the expansion and contraction of space. "Wrapped objects" (*anballages*) have a similar propensity to "open out".

6   A particularly suggestive phrase from Schulz, the title of a section of his *Sanatorium pod Klepsydrą* first published in 1934 and advertised as part of the novel to be called *The Messiah*.

7   The bizarre title admits several translations.

8   This was a huge folding chair and a Canute-like warning to the sea to "go back".

9   Around this time Kantor became enamoured of the umbrella as a shape which could expand and contract to fill "reality", as well as shielding one from dangerous natural interventions.

10   Towards the end of the seventies, Kantor gave a repeat performance of his wartime production in the Bagatela Theatre in Kraków.

11   See Chapter 2, note 3, p. 29.

6

A GRIPPING SÉANCE

Dead Class

When the historic wrought-iron gate finally gives way before the obstinate crowd, the unexpected happens.[1] Instead of quickly taking up the seats they had fought so fiercely for, the fortunate individuals who had thrust their way to the head of the queue simply stand rooted to the spot. The chatter of the large crowd, magnified by the vaulted ceiling of the Krzysztofory Gallery, dies down. In the dim light of the cellar, in a space between the rows of seats and a collection of benches, is the sort of image you tend to see in nightmares: the image of man regressing to his schooldays. On those little wooden benches, littered with the debris of dusty school books, sitting frozen to the spot in the strangest attitudes and staring motionlessly at the people coming in, are old women and old men. Their black clothes, all cut in the same fashion, are reminiscent both of school uniforms and rustic mourning. This is how Kantor's performance starts.

No sooner have the startled spectators taken up their seats in their far-flung parts of the auditorium, than another image makes its appearance, continuing the dream effect. Just as one of the old men raises his finger, rousing himself to answer a question, another takes advantage of the opportunity to thrust his hand out, groaning to show how badly his bladder aches. And that is how it begins, with an air of schoolboy rivalry, this "pantomime of erect fingers". Each one's irresistible urge to score a victory over his classmates leads to a gradual retreat from the benches, and finally to the withdrawal of the entire class. In this succession of movements, the spectator is able to make the startling observation that among the dozen or so participants, there are a couple of people who are paralysed and dependent on friends to move about; their existence is restricted to the mechanical repetition of actions which are "predetermined" for them by their environment.

An interval, allowing the spectators to draw breath, does not last long. At a signal from Kantor, who presides over the whole thing and controls the action like an orchestral conductor, the musical motif of the *Valse François*[2] rings out, ebbing and flowing in step with the memories which draw closer and then move away. Out of the dark doorway of the cellar storeroom comes the procession of elders carrying the corpses of children with them. These figures, already familiar to us, grow to the dimensions of human figures, but have ingrown physically with the bodies they carry. The monstrous "growths" are themselves like children, or – as Kantor says – "their larvae,

13. The school lesson from *Dead Class*. Photo: Jacek Barcz

which store up their entire memory of childhood, rejected and forgotten out of insensitivity, because of the remorseless practicality of everyday life, which deprives us of the means of grasping our lives as a whole." The rhythm of the procession grows faster and faster, repeating itself ad infinitum with gestures fitting each individual, leading them all towards paroxysms of "rapture" followed by total collapse and helplessness. When the Old Folk, in a state of terminal exhaustion, make for the respite of the benches with their last burst of energy, the spectators have been completely drawn into the mood of Kantor's séance, because dream-poetics and oneiric "reality" are crucial to the workings of his performance.

The nightmare goes on: the Old Folk, roused into expressing themselves, jumble together concepts from all over the place. The Bible is mixed up with secular history, the Old Testament with Greek myths. An ultra-punctilious grammar lesson leads to a series of phonological howlers, and the hapless pupils are subjected to even more punishment. These punishments are freely accepted by the multitude as the stigmata of their defects, which are at one and the same time their distinguishing feature. As a tribute to this, Kantor has given each of the protagonists a name with a meaning; the woman showing off her breasts and thighs is the Prostitute-Lunatic; the old woman holding a pane of glass and from behind it heaping abuse on all and sundry is the Lady Behind the Window, as well as being the Crook-backed Year Repeater and Paralytic. The self-referentiality of the whole crowd is underlined by the Charlady and the Beadle from the Good Old Days. These two keep an eye on the spiritual and physical conduct of the eternal students. The Beadle, a familiar figure in Galician schools, has been granted, as it were, two kinds of existence. Wavering on the borders of life, he is at one moment a powerless puppet, while at another he comes back to life, endlessly chanting the Franz Joseph *Hymn to the Habsburg Monarchy*. The Charlady, who represents the so-called *Putzfrau* whose job is simply to keep the school clean, turns eventually into the figure of death.

This is one of the levels in which Kantor introduces the presiding genius of Schulz, who has been, as it were, "invited to participate in the proceedings". What Schulz felt and wrote, Kantor shows and develops.

Schulz's *Treatise on Mannequins* is invoked at this point because the resemblance of the human body to a material object via – as Schulz tells us – "the essence of materiality stripped of all traces of psychic life" leads inevitably to the creation of the mannequin. The school museum of plaster casts, the panopticon, the shows on *The Street of Crocodiles* – these are all images of mannequins from *Cinnamon Shops*,[3] mannequins which, making a show of life, preserve (in contradistinction to this life) the immobility of the image. This is one feature of Schulz's conception. The other is the fleshliness of woman, who, for the author of *The Sanatorium under the Sign of the Hourglass*, is already by nature something like a mannequin. And a third point. "We are fascinated", says the Father in *Treatise on Mannequins*, "by the cheapness, the trashiness, the tawdriness of material."

There is one scene in the production which bears witness to Kantor's impeccable ear. It is the moment when the Lady Behind the Window says, "Go forth and play, my children," and the *Valse François* erupts in all its frenzy. The Old Folk lay hold of their satchels and run round the benches at an elated trot which (like the preceding "flights") ends in a shameless tumble. This scene is the quintessence of Schulz's sensual vision, an act of homage to anti-constructivism.

14. The Beadle from *Dead Class* keeps an eye on the spiritual and physical conduct of the "eternal pupils." Photo: Jacek Barcz

The other "participant" in the performance is Witkiewicz. When the Outsider appears on the school benches, this is the cue for *Tumour Brainard* to make an appearance. This text hardly exists in the performance; its function is to bring out the tension between two realities. The Old Man from the Lavatory becomes Tumour Brainard, the Old Man with the Bicycle is his father, the Woman with the Mechanical Cradle is Rozhulantyna, and the Prostitute-Lunatic is Izia. Witkiewicz's text doesn't fulfil any kind of dramatic function, it simply lends support to the character studies of the protagonists, helping to extend these stereotypes to the point of stripping their gestures of the last shred of significance. The gallop of the Old Man Exhibitionist, motivated by absolutely nothing; the fall of the Old Man from the Lavatory, along with his victims; the wavering of the Woman on the Swing; the self-advertisement of the Outsider – all this echoes the plot of *Tumour Brainard*. In Kantor's performance they have been branded with the "arrested gesture" which traps each of the characters, and which will never reach completion. The Theatre of Automata, kept under surveillance by the old Charlady who has got fat in the meantime, and has been set up as a whoremonger, has turned into a terminal image arrested and set in motion ad lib by Kantor and repeated ad infinitum.

This is how Kantor puts his Theatre of Death manifesto into practice, turning the mannequin, "distorted by its powerful response to death", into a model for the living actor to imitate. Its significance lies not just in a reminiscence of lost youth, its life sacrificed to the grown-ups; not just nostalgia for the values which history has annihilated; and not just in a corresponding understanding of the boundaries of the work of art. It leads also to a break with many of the slogans which have always been accepted as typically avant-garde. Kantor, whose

15. At a sign from Kantor, the *Valse François* resounds. And the procession of Old Folk pours out, humping along the corpses of children. Photo: Jacek Szmuc

16. In Kantor's *Dead Class*, echoes of the plot of *Tumour Brainard* are branded with the "arrested gesture" which traps each of the characters. Photo: Jacek Barcz

accomplishments in the domain of the "open form" work of art always made him nervous and uncomfortable, everlastingly dissatisfied with his achievements, exhibited in this instance the sensitivity of the artist who has taken to heart the question of art's ongoing development. And his artistic declarations of faith against facile, generalised avant-gardism form the fundamental value system of Cricot 2 productions. This value is all the greater because it works on the most intimate levels of experience in everyone.

Notes

1   No-one who was not in Eastern Europe in the Communist period can know the excitement of waiting in a restless queue for some scarce commodity. This included theatre, where one might catch a glimpse of a true image of oneself or the world, a seductive inner gleam to set against the blandness of the outside world. This is what lies behind the cryptic allusion to the heavy gate of the krzysztofory cellar-theatre. Kantor made deliberate use of this for purely theatrical purposes, in keeping with his theories about the appropriation of ready-made reality.

2   Actually Kantor had his sound engineer take care of the musical effects, which were most effective and often evoked Polish fantasies of pre-war extravagance. *Valse François*, also known as *Walczyk Babuni* (Grandmama's Waltz), was a constant feature in family song books.

3   Bruno Schulz has already been evoked in these pages as a great modernist Jewish writer, and a major source of inspiration for Kantor. The collection called originally *Cinnamon Shops* (1934) now forms the substance of *The Street of Crocodiles*. The name seems to have been changed because of the obscurity of the "cinnamon" allusion, which refers to what are (or were) called in Polish *towary kolonialne*, "colonial goods", including spices like cinnamon. However, Schulz made it clear that the primary sense of "cinnamon" here referred not to the spice but to the colour of the shop walls, painted a sort of dirty brown. *Cinnamon Shops* is a set of masterly fables of the strangely creative stagnation of provincial Polish-Jewish life.

7

AROUND THE WORLD WITH
DEAD CLASS

The glamour of foreign successes generally provoked a response among audiences back home, starved as they were of large-scale artistic events. They provoked more and more amazement, and more and more suspicion. This wasn't surprising when nearly every trip abroad by a Polish theatre company was greeted with superlatives. Modest hints at their successes bore witness to

17. A page from the *Daily Haszawua* (Tel Aviv), 15 December 1985. Photo: Jacek Barcz

artistic "triumphs", intellectual "expansiveness", or formal "innovation", "astounding" foreign audiences and bringing them to their knees. It is a pity these impressions were not always subsequently confirmed by the press, which occasionally reported complete flops, as it did with a Polish group visiting Mexico. Suffice it to say that no-one really cared enough to show domestic punters the objective truth: neither the Ministry of Culture, which sent them, nor the *Pagart*[1] agency, which handled the trip, nor the critics, who did make the effort to get on friendly terms with the theatre and understood their difficulties, nor – obviously – the theatre itself, whose trip had to boost its reputation.

Kantor in the British Isles (1976)

In August and September 1976, the Kraków theatre Cricot 2 visited Great Britain, giving 26 performances before an international audience at the 30th Edinburgh Festival; a Welsh audience at the Cardiff University Centre; and the London Society of Connoisseurs. Two fliers, *Kantor is Coming*, and *Kantor Extended*, were distributed all over Edinburgh and London to meet the massive interest in the Polish group, supplementing the voices of the British press.

Voice One:
First Impression

Polish painter-theatre director Kantor has conducted a furious show of fantastic shapes and bizzare connotations consisting of a stunning sequence of dream-like images evoking a forgotten era. The audience enter to confront a pre-1914 mid-European school class of waxworks in stiff black and white garb, sitting behind fusty desks. With fixed expressions they stare at us with the glazed knowledge of a nightmarish world. Suddenly, with a thunderous music, the "dummies" arise, and under the quizzical eye of their mentor Kantor, enact their ritualised education. The figures erupt in the space, one with a bicycle attached to his leg, another with a window pressed anxiously to her face, a third yields a bare breast. Marching and whispering, they arise and subside rhythmically, anarchically enacting their ferocious rituals of birth and death. Kantor has painted an imagistic canvas of theatre which must be seen.

Ann McFerran, review of *Dead Class*, *Time Out*, 10–16
September 1976, p.16. ©Time Out Magazine Ltd.

Voice Two:
The Realm of
"Brutal Comedy"

Although the dead class begins in the schoolroom, it does not end there. Although the lifeless education which they are receiving remains the primary metaphor, Kantor is evoking a lost world of European culture. The school beadle sings the Austrian national anthem, following the news that the Crown Prince has been murdered at Sarajevo.[2] A surging waltz disrupts the class, and from behind a window someone stares. What is that window? What is the suspicion, the alienation which it seems to contain, of prying eyes separated from life by a partition of impregnable glass? Is it the past looking at us, or death in waiting, or simply a mother checking to see whose knees are bloodied today? . . . the impact of the *Dead Class*, another unforgettable production, is indeed like communing with a ghostly world, familiar, but farther from us than the moon . . . The interest of the *Dead Class* is also technical. There is a vein of savage comedy in mid-European drama which we can find in Wedekind, Brecht, Toller and others which we have never managed to realise in this country. It may be lucky that we cannot do so, for we may not have suffered those experiences . . . Kantor shows us, with a shudder, what we are missing."

John Elsom, "Décor by Babel",
The Listener, 2 September 1976.

Voice Three: Horrific Art

Dead Class posed the same problem about horrific art as the canvases of Max Ernst; one lent to the Festival showing a terrifying landscape peopled by obscene sphinxes . . . The long-nosed, sinister Kantor himself is always on stage, commanding the actors like an orchestral conductor or suddenly flinging out an arm to cue the dreadful menacing tick of a clock, or the sound of a schmalzy cafe waltz whose lilt, promise of some never-fulfilled hope of gaiety, momentarily lights up the shell-shocked faces of poor dotards locked in their obsessions . . . How is it that the horrifying in art such as Ernst's or Kantor's can provide, as Edinburgh did so often this year, pleasure and satisfaction? Because, I suppose, such things drag our buried fears and apprehensions into the open and help us to face and understand them. At least, they make us aware we are not alone.

John Barber, "Digging up Our Buried Years",
The Daily Telegraph, 6 September 1976.
©Telegraph Group Limited, London 1976.

Voice Four: Ossification of the Spirit

The subject, clearly enough, is the ossification of the spirit. The child may be the father of the man – but how does that help if a drab and paralysing society is father of the child? It makes a strangely haunting evening, the most memorable in Reekie . . .

Benedict Nightingale, "Proper Stuff", *New Statesman*,
3 September 1976. ©The New Statesman.

Voice Five: Trouble with Labelling

Whatever this is, it's excellent. You couldn't call it a "happening" or an "event" – these words would offend Kantor . . . It is intensely interesting: it can't be labelled, but it lives in the mind as a strong and cohesive statement largely because of the perfect and convinced manner of its performance.

> A.W., "A Painting Comes Alive", *Glasgow Herald*, 23 August 1976, p.11. ©Glasgow Herald Ltd.

Voice Six: The Group and its Leader

Kantor is served by a marvellous company. There is not one action which fails to be perfectly studied and yet as if made for the first time. It's the perfect example of anti-syzygy – that the most dead are the most alive. Kantor himself stalks the stage – the director as conductor. Constantly controlling, assessing, bringing forth, he adds enormously to the intensity, Prometheus bringing down fire; or is it something more – creation itself, the artist as God?

> Allan Massie: "Theatre of Death", *The Scotsman*, 20 August 1976. ©The Scotsman Publications Ltd.

Voice Seven: Antitheatre

Mr Kantor himself, conducting his work in an offhand yet firm way, is the only recognisably human figure on stage. The distinction between people and dolls is blurred by the jerky movements of both, just as the production closes the gap between schoolchildren and these old relics surrounded by rotting textbooks and taking turns to humiliate each other. Mr Kantor's work is antitheatre. He is attempting to create a new kind of drama, a form that has the abstract qualities of music or sculpture as well as something of the unnerving aspects of a happening.

> John Walker, "Revival of Ben Jonson Masterpiece at Edinburgh Festival", *International Herald Tribune*, 7 September 1976, p.7.

Voice Eight: Light and Dark

The opening restores the very basis of experimental theatre by stating a truth about human life that could not be expressed with such tragic economy in any other way. The contrast between what we were, and what we become; the inescapable persistence of childhood into adult life; the idea of the world as a schoolroom, a place of imposed discipline and humiliation where, to the last gasp, we are hoping to learn something that makes sense of it all. For Kantor and his Kraków audiences there is clearly more to the work than that. Like his other recent productions, it is based on a Witkiewicz text, and also reflects his own early memories of Habsburg Poland.

18. The ear-cleaning sequence from *Dead Class*. Photo: Jacek Barcz

> That side of the production is closed to me; likewise its mobile sculptural props which require the attention of an art critic. Fully accessible to any spectator, however, is the extraordinary sense of past time that arises like long undisturbed dust from that sad little place.
>
> Irving Wardle "The Dead Class", *The Times*,
> 30 August 1976. ©Times Newspapers Ltd.

Eight "voices" (minus the usual incidental compliments and standard expressions of delight) present a wide interpretative spread of eight critical views of *Dead Class*. The single negative one among them is a polemic with Kantor's vision of the world – represented by a reviewer in *The Times*, who was entirely uninterested in this sort of a view of life and art. Suffice it to say that no single theatre person in Britain had enjoyed applause on that scale, or reviews which vied with one another in new intepretative nuances. In order to avoid the word "success", which was rather derided in my introductory remarks, it is enough to say Cricot's British trip was an achievement with real . . . class!

Notes

1   The Polish Artistic Agency. During the Communist regime this organisation had a monopoly on all foreign tours by Polish artists.
2   Poland, even more than other Central European nations, had a way of getting caught up in other people's wars. Kantor is exceptionally alert to the peculiarly alienating effect of this colonial situation.

In the Eyes of the French (1977)

Critical Compliments; or the Road to Paris

The group's success in Nancy in 1977 prepared the way for an invitation to the Autumn Festival in Paris. Hubert Gignoux[1] acclaimed *Dead Class* as the most important event of the Nancy festival, while Henri Chapier,[2] welcoming Cricot to Paris, made use of the opportunity to draw people's attention to Polish theatre as a general phenomenon:

> Polish theatre never ceases to inspire Western directors . . . demonstrating that the socialist system can coexist splendidly with a *recherché* avant-garde.

"It is not my habit to cry 'masterpiece' – wrote the permanent co-editor of the Polish monthly magazine *Teatr* Raymonde Temkine[3] – "but the word just seems to force itself upon you. What Kantor has achieved in *Dead Class* is a masterpiece, beyond any doubt." A commentator for *Le Nouvel Observateur*[4] seconded her, starting her critical note: "This Polish performance is one of the most astounding things you will ever see." *Le Quotidien de Paris's*[2] reviewer added: "There is no way of highlighting with sufficient force the power of this almost wordless performance which brings us face to face with a world which we have never seen before." *Le Figaro*[5] decided that, "The whole thing is not exactly a bundle of fun, but it is certainly amazing, powerful with an uncanny energy, and beautifully judged."

"What is Tadeusz Kantor's theatre like?" asked Michael Boue;[6] and on the pages of *L'Humanité Dimanche* he immediately answered his own question: "Like nothing else you have ever seen. This unprecedented piece slips away entirely from the clutches of criticism." *Politique Hebdomadaire*[7] did its best to make value judgements: "This is a truly terrifying show, especially for those who no longer expect the theatre to tell us anything about ourselves, but who hope rather that it will show us our own tragedy – the tragedy of mortal beings whose lives are a torment to them."

The Spirit of Polishness versus Universality

The last sentence leads us to a topic the French critics dealt with accurately and even-handedly: the dialectic of Polishness and universality in *Dead Class*. Temkine[3] notes, "The performance has a universal message, yet one senses in it an exceptionally powerful trace of Polishness." Mathilde la Bardonnie[8] in *Le Monde* issued a warning: "The spectator who tries to find (on the sheet given out before the performance) the titles of particular episodes will just be a nuisance to their neighbours. Neither the images, nor the thrilling music, require any sort of interpretation."

L'Humanité, however, in the person of Jean-Pierre Leonardini,[9] tips the scale in the direction of universal values:

> To assert that *Dead Class* is acted out in a cultural sphere that is exclusively Polish must at first sight appear highly questionable. However, the centre of gravity of this production, which draws us in towards its characters, is the fact that even the least of its actions is situated in a closed field, which is quite simply the field in which history acts.

Temkine[3] cannot imagine Kantor's session without Schulz's *Treatise on Mannequins* or Gombrowicz' *Ferdydurke*, which he claims is the more or less "inverse image" of *Dead Class*. Other critics, too, surpass themselves in drawing cultural parallels. G.S.[7] of *Politique Hebdomadaire* discloses the "nightmare vision of Kantor in seating old folk bum first in old school benches like refugees from the canvases of Hieronymus Bosch." The reviewer from *Théâtre/Publique*[1] observes that these images of grotesque lamentation oscillate back and forth between Münch and Grosz. Nella Bielski[10] from *Le Matin* situates *Dead Class* in the context of central European culture. "Kantor, like Rimbaud," she writes, "provokes a 'real thrill' vis-a-vis honour and sentiment, feeling and longing. It is this thrill, present during the Mass, at the fair, in both liturgy and circus, that aims to take hold of us and disarm us." The article referred to by Bielski, which wants to see Kantor as one of the very few true representatives of European culture, was quite unabashed in the company of all these cultural dignitaries:

> *Dead Class* is not a work of art about death any more than Dante's *Divine Comedy* is a poem about hell and heaven. Kantor has managed to embody in a metaphor the idea of death as a form of the life of art and of memory.

Classical tragedy or Polish Danse Macabre?

"A contemporary dance of death we can all make use of" – that was Pierre Marcabru's[5] attempt to define *Dead Class*. And keeping her colleague from *Le Figaro* company, Caroline Alexander from *L'Express*[11] fell in with this generic definition, as the title of her review shows: "Kantor's Danse Macabre". *Tribune Socialiste*[12] recognised the "dramatic significance" as so frightening and so surprising that (and this is the main reason) it acquired the grandeur of tragedy. "It is a mournful and startling expressionist mime-drama, discovered by chance, and an especially important painterly vision of the 'degraded world'" – we read in *Le Figaro*.[5] "A Romantic *Weltanschauung*, yet somehow Baroque as well", is what we hear in a clamorous genealogy of the performance as a renewal of the convention of the Danse Macabre. "This ceremony, which we might describe as a journey of initiation" – writes Mathieu Galey;[13] while Michael Boue,[6] in an article entitled "Kantor's Master Class", gives some thought to the fact that "via the events and happenings referred to, delusive phantoms enter the proceedings, throbbing nightmarishly with death and the pulsation of sex . . . " *Le Matin*,[10] which sets out to define the autonomous power in the performance, asserts that "*Dead Class* is very close to poetry, because, like poetry, it exists in its own right, and it tries to defend itself." Yet at the same time the author stresses it is a "magic ceremony, in which people and puppets are subjected to a rhythm like the beating of the heart."

It looks as if the most original voice in all these arguments about the precise nature of the "pigeon-holing" of *Dead Class* is that of Jean-Pierre Leonardini at *L'Humanité*.[9]

The play goes round and round like a squirrel in a wheel without beginning or end. We stand face to face with the *camera obscura* of philosophical determinism to a quite unprecedented degree. Kantor's ontological range bursts all bounds. The symbols he makes use of, economical and spare, bear witness to his appropriation of this domain of death. If, indeed, such a domain does in fact exist, it must surely be run along these lines.

Kantor the Pole runs the Domain of Death

This definition, relating to Kantor's role in his production, and so attempting to define the ideology of the Theatre of Death, has become a typical interpretative bone of contention. "A discreet demiurge? Or perhaps more like the conductor of a dumb orchestra?" asks the author of the article "The Squirrel in its Wheel", very sure of his argument. In the columns of *Théâtre/Publique*[1] you can hear a completely opposite view:

> With smoothed-back hair, in a black suit, and a shirt with a white collar, Kantor looks a bit like a flamenco singer. An exceptional intelligence emanates powerfully from him, not the air of the demiurge, or the puppeteer who pulls the strings of his puppets.

Who, then, is this "man in the black suit, who appears at the beginning of his show, slim, with a bird-like face, recalling by his manner not only the director of a school, but the figure of Antonin Artaud" (*L'Express*),[11] who "remains on stage, untiring and anonymous throughout the entire show, controlling all the actions without a word" (*Le Monde*),[8] who is "present and absent at the same time . . . standing back, lost in thought . . . only occasionally joining in the action, to beat time under the nose of the actor" (*L'Humanité*),[9] who is "so deep within his dream that he is constantly coming back to himself, a bit surprised by the course events have taken" (*Théâtre/Publique*.)?[1]

> "Tadeusz Kantor is a cultured man in the noblest sense of the word . . . Yet he presents himself as some kind of rebel and heretic. He gives evidence of having experienced all sorts of artistic tendencies and schools, without pausing for an instant. His aesthetic is one of permanent revolution whose deadly enemy is the fossilised avant-garde." (*L'émotion immédiate*).[10]
>
> "Kantor is a freebooter waging war against our newfound stability . . . It is precisely in this dispensation of death that he finds the last reply possible, so as to conquer the last fatal sickness of art – conformism. The spectator encounters on stage people who are more or less his or her shadow, but whom s/he experiences as endlessly alien. And that, indeed, is death – Kantor explains – that sudden boundary between beings who once were alike." (*Vent d'est, vent de mort*).[14]
>
> "*Dead Class* comes across to us as the farther shore of a journey through art, poetry, music, and theatre under death's dispensation. But to experience all of this anew, Kantor tempts fate by staking everything on one card. He is afraid of only one thing: the risk of sclerosis. Art must be enigmatic. The spectator cannot simply relax in the shade of the pyramid – he declares. So to reaffirm his own loneliness, he shuffles the cards again, which in *Dead Class* are phrases from Witkiewicz, his fetishised author; with Hassidic songs, and a Jewish cradle song." (*La danse macabre de Kantor*).[11]

"His intuition of death has little to do with its iciness, its rot, its boniness – indissociable attributes of the stereotype of this concept. Through his theatre he expresses something altogether opposite to this, and something exceptionally beautiful." (*L'émotion immédiate*).[10]

Kantor's Actors

"The work of the Cricot group is not easy, and it is open only to people of exceptional courage."

"Cricot 2 had the peculiarity of being not an institution but an artistic group."

Two propositions with an ideological colouring from Fabian Gastelier[14] and Allain Leblanc[15] opened the bag of critical opinions, full of admiration for Kantor's actors and their function in his theatre.

"The men and women of Cricot 2 are – paradoxical as this may sound – superb actors," Mathilde La Bardonnie[8] emphasised. "They are so free and so self-possessed at the same time, so caught up by this relentless mechanism, they act in accordance with their own creative imaginations, because the Master will see his way to accepting all of it."

"Harnessed to the yoke of an unheard-of bodily discipline", the reviewer from *Le Nouvel Observateur*[4] aptly noted, "they keep on trying over and over again to answer the question of what sort of state this experience leaves them in" and *L'Humanité Dimanche*[6] argues, "in each performance, Kantor the Vampire demands sacrifices in the shape of living bodies."

The Reaction of the Spectators

The simplest commentary on the kind of interest Cricot 2 aroused when it performed in Paris is a statistic: the house was packed for two weeks running in the Théâtre Chaillot, even though attendances were generally low in the Paris theatres. Reviews and articles which appeared in the Paris press unanimously stressed this fact. More to the point, several critics made an attempt to evaluate the show via the reactions of the spectators. The most interesting voice among them was published under the meaningful heading, "The Gloomy Charm of the Damned":

Childhood and time are waiting for us there through the looking glass of the incomprehensible. One scrambles up in order to pass through the screen of death, whereupon one finds oneself in this circle . . . Thus the spectator discovers in himself unknown roads and landscapes, which he had never known existed: anxieties, regressions, thoughts and summonses. Weighed down by human misery, shadowed by a searching, untiring irony such as the mannequins carry with them, he cannot exist untouched by this ordeal. Each of us has participated in a mystery which has turned us into someone else. Several of these images will probably stay with us for the rest of our lives. Images of hell and images of beauty, images of the visionary carrying with him "the gloomy charm of the damned".

The Paris Edition of Kantor's Writings

By a favourable turn of events, it happened that just when Cricot 2 was performing at the Spring Festival, Kantor's book *The Theatre of Death* appeared on the shelves of the Paris bookshops. The volume, with a preface by well-known French drama specialist Denis Bablet, a professor at the Sorbonne and collaborator with Peter Brook in the International Centre for Theatre Research, contains Kantor's most important theoretical writings, manifestos, essays, important lectures, and polemical pieces showing his theatrical thinking from the Underground Theatre during the Occupation, and the last manifesto of the *Theatre of Death*, a statement of intent which became both the source and the essential critique of *Dead Class*.

The book was at once in demand, and the beautifully produced *Krzysztofory* and *Foksal* catalogues served as a splendid supplement to the show. The only pity is that the first edition of this book had to appear abroad.

Instead of a Conclusion

The Paris success of Cricot 2, seen through the eyes of the French, confirmed the vitality of Kantor's artistic achievement, and bore witness to the fact that *Dead Class* – along with the principles of the Cricot Theatre – had preserved its original freshness. Kantor, the "devilish philosopher of black and white metaphysics" – as Annie Daubenton[16] called him in a review of the book – the "aggressor" (Michael Boue's[6] name for him), had showed himself to be a true Master.

Notes

1 Hubert Gignoux: "Nancy 77". *Théâtre/Publique* 1977 no. 16–17.
2 Henri Chapier – *Le Quotidien de Paris*, 1977 no. 1077 October 11th. p.13.
3 Raymonde Temkine – theatre column in *Europe*, October 1977, pp.201-202.
4 *Le Nouvel Observateur* 1977 October 10–16th. Author not named.
5 Pierre Marcabru: 'Danse macabre polonais". *Le Figaro*, 1977, October 19th.
6 Michael Boue: "La classe du maître Kantor". *L'Humanitié Dimanche*, 1977, no. 88, October 5–11th.
7 G.S. – theatre column in *Politique Hebdomadaire*, 12–23 October 1977.
8 Mathilde La Bardonnie: "Tadeusz Kantor: Le Maître" – theatre column in *Le Monde*, 1977 no. 10173, October 14th
9 Jean-Pierre, Leonardini: "L'ecureuil sur la roue. Le Polonais Kantor gère l'économie de la mort." *L'Humanité* 1977 no. 10309, October 18th.
10 Nella Bielski: "L'emotion immédiate". *Le Matin*, 1977 no. 197, October 17th.
11 Caroline Alexander: "La danse macabre de Kantor". *L'Express*, 1977 no. 1370 October 10–16, p.80, 82.
12 *Tribune Socialiste*, 13–19 October 1977, no. 757.
13 Mathieu Galey: "La grace obscure des maudits". Ibidem.
14 Fabian Gestelier: "Vent d'est, vent de mort". *Tribune Socialiste*, 1977, no. 758, October 20–28th.
15 Allain Leblanc: "Tadeusz Kantor, un tragique vent d'est". Ibidem.
16 Annie Daubenton: *Les nouvelles littéraires*, 1977, no. 2607, October 26–30th.

Shiraz (1977)

Shiraz – city of potentates and holy fast-days – has today[1] been turned into the presentable public face of the "Bloodless Revolution" of the Pahlavi dynasty in Iran. The ancient Persian capital is situated in the south of the country on the same latitude as Kuwait and Delhi. Every August since 1966, on the command of the wife of the Shah, it has become the centre for a major world Festival of the Arts. Farah Diba[2], who is extremely well equipped to understand contemporary art and its preoccupations, chose Shiraz – famous as the city of Hafiz and Saadi – as the setting for a permanent artistic event designed to bring together the artistic achievements of every continent. So it comes about in the hottest month of summer, among the royal ruins of the fortress in Persepolis, splendid mosques, rose gardens celebrated in song by Saadi, at the tomb of the legendary writer of *gazel*,[3] you may meet a crowd of people speaking many languages, applauding ensembles and artists from all over the world. And you will find the same thing in the concert halls, the specially adapted sports halls-cum-auditoria, and the up-to-date television studios which have been put at the disposal of the festival.

The Shiraz/Persepolis Festival of the Arts is not just a manifestation of a different, Asiatic sensibility, it is also – and this is more interesting – an educational experience for Europeans in how to approach a work of art. The organisers of the festival, representatives of the Iranian cultural elite with western university educations, have forgotten nothing of the centuries-old resources of their own Persian culture, and approach art as a whole, a totality. They are not deluded, as we often are, by specialisations, categories, or whether a thing exists on its own account or in combination with various other branches of art. With their awareness of the fine traditions of oriental culture, and the frenzied pace of the non-stop revolutionary process in contemporary art, they come back, or would like to come back, to the unitary, indivisible nature of art as a basic impulse in man's spiritual life. This is how the festival finds a place for the improvisatory theatre of distant provinces of India, a European avant-garde group, a Japanese puppet theatre, Italian *commedia dell'arte*, South American ritualistic theatre, a French version of free-style dance, a group playing traditional Arab music, a splendid New York orchestral ensemble, a retrospective of Japanese films, and a group of films by Luis Bunuel. Anything festival director, Farrokh Gaffary, regards as worn-out convention or unoriginal imitation has no place here.

There is yet another aspect to this gathering: it can serve to further the ends of Iranian art. A festival of this kind, showcasing artistic developments of the year from around the world, should – as Farah Diba stressed – serve as an inspiration for the development of Iranian art. Indeed successive festivals have inspired an increasing number of energetic proposals from the Iranian hosts. This was the case in 1977 when our hosts decided to stage performances by seven of their own groups.

The participation of Polish groups in the Shiraz Festival has come to be taken for granted. This fact constitutes a recognition and a distinction all the more remarkable in that Poland joins the ranks of the representatives of the "old world". Grotowski, Penderecki and the Kraków Philharmonic, Jasiński, Adam Kaczyński with the group MW-2 and Schaeffer, but above all Kantor with Cricot 2 – are our representatives. I say Kantor "above all" because in that year Cricot had received an invitation for the second time[3] (which is against festival rules) and the Shah's wife, in her opening speech, singled out Kantor as the jewel of the festival.

The Cricot group put on *Dead Class* in Shiraz: a production which had been tried and tested in Poland (Kraków, Łódź, Wrocław, Warsaw), and in Europe (Edinburgh, London, Amsterdam, Nüremberg). What struck the group most was not so much the ovations of the overflowing audience, as the endless discussions aimed at translating into oriental terms of reference the significance of Kantor's ambiguous vision; his "vivisection" of man's fate in the context of a particular historical combination of circumstances.

The critical commentaries in two Teheran newspapers communicate the special air of fascination that surrounded the Polish offerings. The reviewer in the *Teheran Journal* (23 August 1977) began his description of the performance: "Tadeusz Kantor's *Dead Class* swept the audience off its feet by the brilliance of its staging and the striking fervour with which the actors expressed the impotence of humanity in its hopeless dash towards its fate." Soumaya Saikali, theatrical editor of *Kayhan International* (25 August 1977), highlighted the following points:

> Basic values and actions are interrogated. Death, shame, sex, the degradation and disintegration of all of this, together with its pathos and a premonition of the absolute, are so organically intertwined that the swirl of a lovely loud waltz from this fairground roundabout can show us that all this would happen equally well either in pre-war Poland or anywhere, any time.
>
> So much is communicated in this electrifying art, as if it wanted to turn into some sensual bundle of nerves. The audience, rooted to the spot, is so powerfully engaged that it is given the opportunity to compare its own past with the one that is being presented. The stage is full and engrossing. Everyone felt that he or she was drawn into a greater whole from the moment when the actors, in their tireless activity, juggled with roles and objects in an almost magical style.

The success of Cricot 2 at the Third Festival of Art in Shiraz was underlined by the unofficial discussions, and the official meetings and receptions, given in honour of Kantor and his group.

There is an old Persian proverb, "Let the stranger into your house, but do not let him leave". Kantor's stay in Shiraz, and the conduct of the hosts towards their Polish guests, are yet another example of the wisdom of the old maxim.

Notes

1 This evocation of the Shah's Iran just before the Islamic Revolution has acquired a unique historical value.
2 Author of *The Rose Garden*, a book of poetry.
3 A poetic form developed by Hafiz and used by Persian poets.
4 *Lovelies and Dowdies* was performed at the Shiraz Festival in 1974.

New York (1979)

The visit of Kantor's Kraków group to New York had a double significance. For American audiences, it ratified the findings of the poll in *Newsweek*, which acclaimed *Dead Class* after it was shown in London in 1976 as the finest production in the world. For the Polish group it provided an opportunity to break into the American art scene, which is notoriously unreceptive and unsympathetic to Europeans. The only Poles to successfully break down this barrier have been Polański, Penderecki, and Grotowski.

The sixteen performances of *Dead Class* at La Mama's by now legendary place on East 4th Street proved that despite a series of unpropitious circumstances, like the startling temperature of 30°C below, the terrible atmosphere that resulted from Pagart's[1] failure to sign the contract with Ellen Stewart, and the almost total lack of publicity by La Mama, Kantor and his group had built a reputation on their theatrical revelations of the last few seasons. *The Los Angeles Times* complained that the group had performed only in New York, without visiting the West Coast. This was a compliment that had not been paid to a non-American group in a long time.

As Cricot had grown accustomed to a series of triumphs in international festivals and artistic events throughout the world, the sparse attendance at some performances in the first week gave rise to speculation about the impermeability of the American scene. But in the following two weeks there was an audience that would have sufficed for half a year. The reviews in the New York press were the decisive factor.

An avalanche of reviews was set off by the *New York Times* on 3 July with an article by Richard Eder, cited many times in the Polish press, entitled "Polish Avant-gardists at La Mama". It is worth recalling quotations which have not yet been exploited:

> Art has arisen in the mind of Mr Kantor, but only its shadows reach us, the pathetic Platonic troglodytes. The extensive text in the programme, translated from the Polish into something supremely incomprehensible, informs us that: "It would be groundless pedantry to try to uncover all the hidden links in the chain which are needed in order to understand the action of this play in its entirety." This sounds somewhat hermetic and pretentious. What we saw was certainly hermetic, full of repetitions, offering no opportunities to unearth the archetypes of what remained. But it was not in the least pretentious. Here we have a strength and beauty of imagery, a precision and absolute mastery of artistic expression . . . The play or séance, whatever you want to call it, consists of a series of short sequences, in the course of which various individuals, groups, and sometimes the whole class, leave their places at their benches . . . The atmosphere undergoes a succession of changes – from apathy to hysteria. These hysterical outbursts are in Polish, and from time to time they rebound off our sensibilities, with the obvious proviso that the significance of this production resides in the movement and expressiveness of individual characters: and in particular that each of the performers exploits the strength of his or her personality.

To get the feel of the atmosphere which surrounded the visit of Cricot 2 up to the time of the first reviews, two announcements may be cited together. A *Polish Week* article (28–29 January 1979), under the "Cultural Events", urged emigré Poles to see "what is, without a doubt, the most celebrated production to come out of Poland since Grotowski's *Apocalypsis cum Figuris*."[2] Helen Szmuness, after quoting from a discussion about *Dead Class* in *Dialog*,[3] confronted her readers with the following conclusion:

> For sure, a performance which manages to convey to us such a cargo not so much of art as of "the world", justifies the three years spent waiting for a chance to see it. We have to come straight out with it: Kantor's production will not be equally well received by all spectators. It does require a certain sort of concentration, and what one might call "theatre culture", or perhaps just the willingness to confront a different sort of theatre than we are used to on the whole in America. For this reason, I have some hesitation in recommending it to those readers who go to the theatre to unwind and to relax.

Listing the complete run of New York shows in his essay in the bi-weekly *Other Stages*, Glenn Loney – who had seen the play already in Edinburgh in 1976 – egged Americans on in the following terms:

> It isn't easy to move about with Edward Gordon Craig on your back, especially since the time Craig died. But this is no problem for an outstanding artist – a director like Tadeusz. For Kantor the Craig burden which he bears is metaphorical, spiritual, intellectual. His actors, on the other hand, in the "Cricot-2" company from Kraków, have to hump about this material baggage of death, which real life has given shape to. But in *Dead Class*, which has been on for three weeks at La Mama, all of them, and the characters they are playing as well, are dead. Whence comes this fascination with death? Is this by any chance from the same gangrened artery, connected to that same poisoned heart, that gave us the cold ironies of Polański's *Dance of the Vampires* or the tempestuous theatricality of Grotowski's Poor Theatre? For anyone struggling to distance themselves from such tormenting thoughts, the obsessive vision of Kantor's *Dead Class* might look like just one more contribution to the genre of the "Polish joke". But this really is not the case. What we are talking about is the very serious business of death.

The *SoHo Weekly News*, which took the New York run of *Dead Class* very seriously, devoted two weighty essays to it: the first of these proclaimed, "First night of *Dead Class* by Cricot 2 at La Mama is the Great Event of the Year in the avant-garde theatre."

Tish Dace, in her article "The Class of the Living Death" (*SoHo Weekly News*, 15 February 1979), enthused over the "performers of *Dead Class*, this group of travelling professionals with amazing discipline, coordination, vocal and physical dexterity, and an expressivity only comparable to that of the leading American groups"; and argued that the universality of the language of the performance was intelligible to every spectator, regardless of national peculiarities or linguistic barriers.

An analytical account of the actors' style led Dace to the following conclusions:

> This kind of non-representational style of acting and production is by no means synonymous with abstraction: Kantor opposes abstraction as emphatically as he opposes the theatre's mechanical apparatus for the duplication or the simple presentation of the real world. If verisimilitude is no criterion of his work, neither is any sort of bloodless idea, or any antihumanistic proposal to concretise the

19. *Dead Class* at La Mama, New York, 1979. Photo: Jacek Barcz

consciousness and the life of the actor. Although he uses dummies, he does this so discreetly as to run counter to Craig's dictum that the "marionette" in the theatre is more important than the human subject.

William Harris, a week later, in the same cultural journal, cited the experiments of the Underground Theatre and speculated about the Polish context of Kantor's work:

> This theatre is a theatre of destruction and devastation . . . it outstrips the codification of ideas that we find in Grotowski. Mention of Grotowski irritates Kantor. He describes his fellow director – without malice, but with the same inner conviction which coloured our opening exchanges – as a charlatan. Kantor is, at one and the same time, supercilious, and ready to leap to the defence of his own research, the greater part of which is perfectly intelligible to a New York audience. Just like Richard Foreman, who directs his own ontological-hysterical scenario from the proscenium, Kantor "directs the traffic" during the course of the performance. Forever on the edge of the theatrical space there is a magician and secret agent rolled into one . . .

Kantor could not abide the majority of European experiments because of their resolute humourlessness. "To live without a sense of humour is to live unintelligently."

Harris's reasoning points to one outcome:

> In *Dead Class* Kantor has constructed a single (in its way) universal and very commodious metaphor – of a class with its raw, simple benches – in order to offer the imagination a correlative of his mainly satirical vision of the human condition.

The point made by this review in *The SoHo News* can be developed with the help of Merle Ginsberg's findings in the *Villager* (19 February 1979):

> *Dead Class* may be understood as a metaphor on several levels – the class as life, adults as children, learning as fascism ... *Dead Class* is magical, dark, and as exciting as childbirth – a lesson in life, Edvard Munch for the stage.

The title of the piece in the *Villager*, "Poland's incomparable 'Theatre of Death': a Matter of Life and Death", was developed in the text as follows:

> *Dead Class* is such a monumental and serious piece of work, that it would be foolish to hail it as the theatrical event of the New York season – a performance like this simply cannot be compared with anything. *Dead Class* aims to stun and upset its audience with an image: this is painting brought to life by events. Kantor and his group are closer in their work to painting and sculpture than to the theatre. For this reason *Dead Class* too, as a work of art, is aimed at creating a scenic space somewhere in between the canvas and the proscenium, the photograph and the dais.

Eileen Blumenthal's review ("Haunted by History", *Village Voice*, 26

20. Tadeusz Kantor. Photo: Jacek Bogucki

February 1979) explores the Polish-Jewish archetypes contained within Kantor's vision, and realistic fragments from cultural and religious enclaves which no longer exist; then tries to bracket *Dead Class* with Grotowski's experiments, concluding:

> "The work of Cricot-2 cannot be evaluated in terms of Grotowski's theories. Everything taking place on stage is truly admirable. Kantor's imagination has a freshness and strength such as I have only rarely, and a while ago, seen in the work of the Open Theatre, Grotowski, and Winston Tong."

The New York reviewers largely avoided stereotypical descriptions of Kantor's dramatic sessions, and refrained from regurgitating citations from his writings. All tended towards the conclusion expressed with particular brevity by Marylin Stasio in the *New York Post* (21 February 1979). The last paragraph of the review, "*Dead Class* is dynamite – a real triumph for the avant-garde," reads:

> Everything the actors do captivates our thoughts. Our imagination is ensnared by the importunate eyes of the characters, who wear themselves out in a clownish game with their own childhood ... who know that they have been condemned in advance to repeat in death the mistakes they made in life. As a political metaphor, *Dead Class* is annihilating. As an existential reflection on life, it is deeply disturbing. As a theatrical event – it is dynamite.

Notes

1 Pagart (*Polish Artistic Agency*) – see note 1, p. 46.
2 Jerzy Grotowski (1933–1999) initially perhaps made more impact internationally than Kantor, based as much upon his ideas about the theatre as upon his creative work. This was probably because Grotowski was close to Peter Brook and other well-known exponents of the "empty space" school of theatre, and his minimalist theories were formed from eclectic and spiritual writings which also fed alternative culture in the west. Kantor, by contrast, deals in "dense" modernist spaces full of cultural and artistic allusions and intertexts, and seems to eschew the attractively youthful workshop approach of Grotowski. Where Kantor moved towards theatre-as-carnival, Grotowski moved towards theatre-as-therapy-and-ritual.
3 *Dialog* was, and still is, the foremost Polish theatrical journal. Despite being founded in 1956 under the Communist regime, it was always considered a remarkably well-informed straight-talking and professional journal, uncompromised by political expediency.

Toga-mura and Tokyo (1982)

Kantor's theatrical "séance", acclaimed by the Kraków public on 15 November 1975, had become a phenomenon in the world history of theatrical reception. Cricot 2 flew to Japan from Warsaw on Sunday, 25 June 1982, the twentieth country in a row in which Kantor was directing *Dead Class*. Toga-mura and Tokyo were, in succession, acting as hosts for the show which seemed to have won every award from the notice in *Newsweek* in 1976 to the off-Broadway award of the OBIE in 1979.

Japan was going to be tough, starting with the perennial difficulties posed by Pagart,[1] famous for hindering artists rather than helping them. Then, clarifying the terms of our invitation, we had to enlighten the organisers on the structure of Cricot 2 (which was unknown on the continent of Europe) and Kantor's requirements, springing from this. Kantor never capitulated when confronted by bureaucratic managerial thinking. The journey presented its own dangers, covering nineteen thousand kilometers in over thirty hours. Japan is seven hours ahead of Poland, and the temperature in summer reaches 40°C, with a very high humidity.

Cricot, inured to transcontinental travel and conflicts with various rich benefactors, reached the first stage of its journey on Tuesday, 27 June. The first objective was Toga-mura . . . a village located in a depression between the hills, which cuts off the ports of the Sea of Japan in the middle of the biggest island – Honshu. Making the most of the tranquillity of the setting, 1200 km as the crow flies from Tokyo, it was here that the supremo of the event, Tadashi Suzuki, decided to organise the First International Theatre Festival.

Suzuki, Japan's second most famous theatrical avant-gardist after Shuji Terayama (of the Tenjo Sajiki Theatre), conjured into existence in Toga-mura a drama centre which made full use of the splendid surroundings. Devoting itself to working with his own method, coupling the experiments of the European avant-garde with the traditional acting values of Japanese theatre, Suzuki made every effort to include the Kraków group among the group of ten invited.

Presenting their offerings twice for the benefit of the theatre-going public from the big cities, the ten were Cricot 2, Waseda Sho-Gekijo Japan, Tenjo Sejiki, the centuries-old traditional Noh and Kyogen theatre groups, two avant-garde American theatres led by Robert Wilson and Meredith Monk, the world-famous Indian group from Kerala, a dance theatre from Bhutan, and the shockingly confrontational British street theatre group Welfare State International. The ensembles were able to make use of either the open-air theatre or the Noh Theatre, which had been reconstructed in accordance with the rules of Noh, seating about 300 people. Cricot 2 staged *Dead Class* in this cramped space, making good use of the blackness of the surroundings. This worked well with the gloomy, disturbing mood evoked by recollections of school classrooms, poor and degraded by inhuman stretches of time and human manipulativeness.

Five days in Toga-mura meant not only acclimatisation, but also two productions preceded by full-scale rehearsals. A press conference with numerous journalists, critics, and four television crews, was just the beginning of a psychological battle with . . . the frenzied elements. It so happened that this spring the rainy season had lasted a little longer than usual, and it rained heavily for half a day. The typhoon which had flooded Nagasaki around 20 July was now threatening Honshu, in the vicinity of our route from Togamura to Tokyo. A ghastly night, endured by Poles who were quite unused to such fierce gusts of wind, was evidence that we had landed on the tail of a typhoon.

A dozen or so days performing on the boards of the Tokyo Space Parco 3, one of the theatres belonging to the well-known Seibu chain of supermarkets in Shibuya – a district famous from the Olympic Games of 1964 – lent a happier perspective to everything. It meant a sudden leap from the quiet of the Japanese mountains to the traffic that roared chock-a-block day and night, the bright lights, the human ants scurrying by, the moloch that was one of the biggest conurbations in the world. The Kraków ensemble performed *Dead Class* here eight times, and the major television station NHK recorded the whole performance, compiling a ninety-minute programme designed to

21. Tadeusz Kantor. Photo: Jacek Bogucki

22. Tadeusz Kantor. Photo: Jacek Bogucki

precede Kantor's performance on 26 September. Kantor agreed to give a limited number of interviews, and took part in a seminar organised by Terayama, devoted to his concept of theatre. Kantor's business-like discussions with publishers there prepared solid ground for a repeat invitation to Japan. This arose from a number of reliable sources, unperturbed by two earth tremors we experienced before lunch, and at night.

The Japanese received *Dead Class* very well. Some extracts from the reviews in two of the most important Japanese journals. *Asahi Shimbun* and *Yomiuri Shimbun*, bear witness to this. Since I do not wish to be accused of linguistic charlatanism, I freely admit I was helped in translating these reviews by my friend Wiesław Romanowski, designer and programmer, graduate and doctor of Tokyo University, victor in four oratory competitions in Japanese, known to viewers from the television programme of Bohdan Wojtczak: a Szczecin engineer who failed to find work at Szczecin Polytechnic after graduating!

> What sort of attraction can this kind of stage have? Bitterness, sadness, suffering, horror, but also an original sort of beauty and a wealth of humour. A microcosm, a space bounded by light, into which people have been inserted in order to lend it larger social and historical dimensions.

This was how *Asahi Shimbun* began its review (5 August 1982), preparing for a statement of the universality of *Dead Class*'s message, "Kantor's production is the kind of art that asks wide-ranging questions about the meaning of life".

Yomiuri Shimbun (in the person of Professor Takahashi, an English specialist from Tokyo University) tried to discover a political context in which to locate an interpretation of the Polish national spirit, betokened in the title, "The bitterness and anger of the fatherland transposed to the level of art": "One of the factors that has contributed to the painfully oppressive atmosphere of the production is the fact that the spectator is, willy-nilly, bound to perceive there, as one of its ingredients, the bitter national history of the fatherland, Poland."

Yasunari Takahashi tells us in the columns of *Yomiuri Shimbun* (6 August 1982):

> Yet one cannot unambiguously assert that the anger and bitterness of a nation which has repeatedly found itself the prey of a barbaric imperial thirst for conquest is unequivocally woven into the performance. Nevertheless, two scenes provide evidence of this fact. The first is when the character rising from the dead sings the Austrian national anthem with such hatred; the second is where the old folk exit, to dance a waltz out of pure cussedness, containing all the prewar symbolism of *la belle époque*. In these scenes it is difficult not to see and to hear the voice of stifled anger and bitterness bursting in a great cry from the soul of the nation.

We felt great pride that our intentions and meaning were understood in this way. Our encounter with Japanese civilisation signified to us that art may be the only area in which world nations can compete with the Japanese. This trip bore witness to the fact that Poland was lucky to have Kantor, and could glory in his art without feeling the need to build a "Second Japan".[2]

Notes

1   Pagart – see note 1 on page 51.
2   This is an allusion to Lech Wałęsa's loudly proclaimed fascination with Japan. The President of Poland and former Solidarity leader was so impressed with Japan's economic development that he proposed the following motto, "Let's build a Second Japan".

8

KANTOR IN OPPOSITION
TO HIMSELF

(Conversation, July 1980)

KM: Most *Dead Class* spectators come out of the performance believing it to be an unrepeatable event, a work of art enclosed within itself and "finished". Critics likewise have been prepared to swear that it is a "summit" marking the end of an era in Cricot's investigations, and the crowning achievement for you and your company. The world reception of *Dead Class*: applause, homage, adoration, prizes, repeated invitations, endless discussions, new interpretations, analyses, reviews, notices – all serve to bear out the claim that this is your *terminus ad quem*. Yet you have never hesitated to take the next step forward. *Wielopole, Wielopole* is an attempt to "leapfrog" *Dead Class*, and is therefore perhaps one of the riskiest steps of your career.

TK: A natural step, and necessary. Those who are close to me noticed how a sort of "oppositional force" took shape in my mind. It was oppositional – and, by the way, very welcome – because for an artist to be able to accomplish anything in art he has to question his *terminus ad quem*. An artist who believes in his art believes in its development, and the inevitable process of the constant development of his art. The artist has to set the present moment and place in which he finds himself over and against what went before. This is the only thing that gives an artist "go" – at least that's how it is with me. I don't like going on in the same direction, I don't like profiting from some situation or widely acclaimed "success", I don't like cashing in on successes of the past and duplicating them. I consider that a waste of time.

KM: What you have just put in a rather theoretical way is consistent with the feelings of your actors. All of us noticed how the often onerous business of presenting *Dead Class* during those long foreign tours would wind you up out of all proportion.

TK: This was down to the demands of our tours, when we tirelessly acceded to the demand for *Dead Class*. And although this process of "duplication" incorporated a modification on each occasion, it was a tedious business for me. It was just a question of bowing to the inevitable. And every modification, every change served only as an injection of freshness into the rather hidebound structure of the performance . . .

KM: It seems to me that these alterations, connected to some extent with changes in casting, played a decisive role in different versions of the production, different mutations of *Dead Class*.

TK: Perhaps you are right, but I would really have to think hard about whether or not those "mutations" – as you call them – were really changes at the level of ideas.

KM: Your work on *Dead Class* – daily, tireless work – and your vacillations, are for me a way of understanding the paradox which the "exploitation" of *Dead Class* threw into relief. It resides in the diametrically opposed requirements of the creative artist and the recipient. While the audience demanded one performance after another, you, as "author", were growing increasingly irritated and upset – it was all quite simply unnecessary, from your point of view.

TK: I can tell you straight that I have no further need for a production after I have created it, and the first night marks the end of my creative involvement. Perhaps the actor goes on creating, but this is rare. The problem of the process of creating, and the work of art which results from this process, comprises a serious dilemma, since it touches upon a terrible cultural habit which has come to seem natural. The act of writing a book, composing a symphony, painting a picture, is recognised as a creative process, an exceptional revelation of the power of the human spirit. So it is surprising that the apprehension of this exceptional phenomenon comes about only *after* it has been extinguished. Only the product is consumed, in the form of a book, or a finished work of art, or a picture hung in a gallery; the creative process itself remains completely inaccessible. To express this more vividly, we might say that in the reception of the work of art, paradoxically, the most inspiring, the most spiritual moment has been expunged. That is art's great mystery; only the trace of this process remains, to be exhibited, consumed. We try to discover in this "imprint" some reflection of the great explosion which occurs during the process of artistic creation, but all our efforts are in vain. There was a time when I thought that this discovery process had a sort of radiant inevitability in itself. The result was the *Popular Show* of 1963. The work of art – the product of the creative process – then seemed to me to be of dubious validity, too "official", and I decided to present it as an image assiduously effaced from memory, removed from the gaze of the spectators so as to lose nothing of its *value*, as the work of art had virtually become a monument. I counted as art everything conforming to that turbulent and gloomy era, all those little details – however unrefined, unrepresentative, embarrassing, nonsensical, or refractory – that comprise the unique and original raw material of creation. I presented everything that went into the process of shaping the work of art.

KM: Did those art experiments of 1963 find an echo in your work for the theatre?

TK: In my view, it mainly bore fruit in Florence during the ninth month of the 1979–1980 rehearsals for *Wielopole, Wielopole*. This was an exceptional period in our work, and highly intensive. I simply could not permit myself, in that context, the kinds of practices I was used to in Kraków. In Kraków, when I was bored with rehearsing, I would often just call a halt for an hour, and the actors I had engaged would take an hour off to voice their complaints. They wanted to let the world know about the conditions of work in the Krzysztofory Gallery; cold, damp, lack of heating. Those breaks, which I called for a variety of reasons, livened up the proceedings considerably. In Florence we worked every day in a frenzied but methodical style, and this produced an exceptionally stressful state of mind. The stresses were so great that the rehearsals – in my view – were extremely interesting. At the beginning of rehearsals we would have a room full of spectators, but would have to ask them to leave because they distracted and annoyed the actors. The mere fact that people had come to the rehearsals was symptomatic. Our efforts fascinated them, especially when they were able to see for themselves how the "creative spark flew". The best example, as far as the audience was concerned, was the Last Supper – the epilogue to the performance. For only the seventh time, I succeeded in creating the effect I had been striving for. Twenty spectators who were watching when the scene took definitive shape were truly overwhelmed by it. My approach to the epilogue sprang from the contradictions contained in the six scenes preceding it, which remained – despite tireless work – unsatisfactory. This was a process lacking in logic and quite absurd; entirely negative and destructive. It was precisely because of this systematic work (over a long period of time) to break down the concepts encoded in the minds of the actors that this fantastic image suddenly emerged. All the previous factitious, cut-and-dried solutions gave way before the result of a spontaneous rehearsal.

KM: Even though you never employed the methods of the "spectacular school" of painting, putting the process of creation on display, your fascination with it obviously goes deeper than the "happening".

TK: I had great respect for this tendency in art more or less from the outset: this way of attaching greater weight to the process itself than to the effect. That was why my academic colleagues insisted that my images lacked the material solidity of the images of the classics. I linked these pastimes to my "mousetrap" project, a technique for catching the attention of spectators in a "trap", which – in itself – becomes the basic creative imperative.

KM: Let's get back to the Florence rehearsals . . .

TK: The experience of Florence and my work on *Wielopole, Wielopole* provides the closest possible parallel to my work as an artist, especially since the spectators at the rehearsals were "programmed" as if they had been former students at my school. I opposed the founding of any such institution from the outset, but undertook open rehearsals which were intended to be a "stratum" of shared enquiry. Through them I wanted to experiment with what I spoke of earlier: the participation of the spectator in the creative process, and their receptivity to this process.

KM: Do you think this process has a place in every sort of theatrical model?

23. *Wielopole, Wielopole*. Preparation for the Last Supper. Photo: Jacek Barcz

TK: Absolutely not – in the "normal" institutional theatre this process is impossible. My kind of theatre works in terms of the resources of the *performance*. One famous director working in conventional theatre invited the public to a rehearsal, with a view to opening up the creative process. But in his own view he made a fundamental mistake. The rehearsal the public attended wasn't really a creative process, because it isn't enough merely by an act of directorial will to decide that a series of rehearsals can in themselves become a work of art, simply by virtue of their "openness". There has to be some artistic structure involved in the actual process. It is fascinating in theory, but exceptionally boring in practice. I was eager to do something like this myself, but I recognised that the testimony, the communication, the message, which my play contains – and which I wish to put across by means of the play – are much more important than any structural discoveries. Working on *Wielopole, Wielopole*, I recognised this fact with all the vividness of an irrevocable choice. What's more, my realisation ran counter to the body of theory I had erected around my performance. I wrote several new manifestos and tried to formulate many definitions – illusion as repetition, the army as the existential condition of the actor, reality and fiction, "the room" and its antechamber as the opposed sites of the action. In the end all this helped me a lot, because without it we would have had a purely illustrative piece of work.

KM: Performance itself is your ideological-artistic statement. What is the context of the theoretical problems you faced?

TK: Let us take spiritualism, even though the word produces in me a reaction of suspicion. I once used to believe in the intellect. But today I
don't know if intellect really was the "gland" that secreted my passion
for the radical avant-garde; or whether it just assumed its own protec-
tive cover or system of defences in the face of the adsurdity of the
postwar world and the muddle-headedness of postwar culture. At any
rate, this idea has helped me through many difficult moments.
Evidently the world is more complex than we supposed. Everything
has started to go rotten in the domain of the intellect. The "heights"
ascribed to reason have started to reveal serious lacunae and deficien-
cies, producing fatal consequences. This applies to life as well as art.

   I think also about the tension between our life and what we may call
"the reality of the antechamber"; the reality "behind the doors", "through
the wall". The disproportion between "the room" and "the ante-room"
is huge. It has always existed, but that room was never so comfortable and
so banal, and the dangers threatening us, the gathering storm piling up in
the antechamber, were never so massive. At the outset, I wanted to set up
a "child's world" in the space behind the door. But when I did this in the
spirit of Schulz's suggestions, I resolved I would be a match for him. I
made an effort to steer clear of all the symbolic representations which the
literary-artistic tradition and the Bible put my way, even though I took
full advantage of these. And that was my position throughout the
rehearsals, and I stood by it strictly and with a full sense of its importance.

24. Kantor and the Recruits in *Wielopole, Wielopole*. Photo: Jacek Barcz

9

BETWEEN ABSOLUTE FORM AND THE REVELATION OF FEELING

Wielopole, Wielopole

In the ordinary, institutional theatre the stage constitutes an incredibly solid foundation. It serves the actors as a place to act, to present, to imitate. The stage is where the actor acquires the status of artist, as well as praise and fame, often without even trying, without having earned it. Regardless of what shape it takes – Italian style, in the round – regardless of what participational model it tries to lay on the audience, the stage remains at all times a passive sanctuary. Canvas serves the painter as the same sort of sanctuary. In the sanctuary of the stage and the sanctuary of the canvas, all things are possible in contemporary art. Here the greatest excesses are enacted, without any retribution.

In the Cricot 2 theatre, in more or less all my productions, I keep coming back to the problem of the imperative need to destroy this artistic space, to exit from the reservation labelled "art". When art decides to leave its reservation and go out into the world, there comes a moment of protracted collision, because art has its own categories, which are not the same as those of life. The happening, all the "activité" and manifestos arising from it, were designed to make art leave its reservation and enter the domain of reality. But if I give up on the artistic "space" constituted by the stage, what have I got left?

Speaking at the rehearsal of *Lovelies and Dowdies*, Kantor here presents perhaps the best definition of the role of artistic space in the Cricot 2 theatre. The spaces Kantor chose for performing his play, however, do not just supply some sort of emotion to an audience exposed to the real-life consequences of one choice rather than another. A body of theory elaborated over several years, and amazingly consistent, decides about each of the places selected, low in real-life status though they are. The whole thing is done in an effort to destroy all the attributes of the theatrical stage: illusion, imitation, and presentation. Dubious places, in real-life terms: a casino, a cloakroom, a waiting room, an antechamber, an attic, make way in the end for a space illuminated by recollections of childhood.

After the schoolhouse of *Dead Class*, Kantor devised as the site of his latest production the room of his childhood. His vision was an attempt to recreate the living quarters of a country-house-cum-presbytery presided over by the priest, Józef Radoniewicz, the uncle-grandfather figure to little Tadeusz. Kantor was brought up there by his mother, who waited in vain for years for the return of her husband from the First World War.

Wielopole Skrzyńskie, where Kantor saw the light of day in 1915, nineteen kilometres from Ropczyce, is situated on the boundary between Pogórze

Ciężkowickie and Kotlina Sandomierska. Its history was shaped by its geography, merchants in the Middle Ages being attracted by its location on a trade route. Subsequently only military strategists took an interest in it, and then only in time of war. The mercantile "invasion" was the main reason for its initial prosperity, which was then effectively destroyed by numerous wars, including the Second World War. Hence the history of Wielopole was one of defeat and downfall, rather than ascent and development.

Approaching Wielopole from the hillocks of Pogórze, the settlement remains hidden in its depression until the last upward step, when the first houses and spires of the churches come into view. The road enters the quadrilateral of the market place, enclosed by old tenement-houses. Viewed from the hill, the church crowns one of these blocks of the market; opposite, the synagogue once stood, and Poles and Jews lived on opposite sides of the square. In the 20th century, Wielopole shared the fate of other Polish-Jewish towns in Galicia, and was forgotten by history. Schulz's drawings for his *Cinnamon Shops*[1] communicate what a stranger felt, visiting Wielopole in 1980 to take in the atmosphere of Kantor's native town.

The room as the focus of the action entered Kantor's work after a long interval. We have to go back to the War, and Kantor's Underground Theatre, to find an equivalent in the Kraków dwelling-places where *Balladyna* and *The Return of Odysseus* were performed. The room in *Wielopole, Wielopole* is quite different, however – the material substance of the wooden floor provides a boundary for an immaterial space. Wood becomes the raw timber from which all the component parts of the spectacle are made, including those which are indispensable for bringing the room to life, such as the windows and doors. These elements are mobile, we can shift them, replace them, or substitute one for another at will. By these means Kantor seems to want to provide a medium for the illusoriness of "truth-to-memory". This gives rise to the comic situation in which each of the protagonists tries to hold on to his vision of a common family room. The household fixtures and fittings, alternately produced and removed, the table with its chairs and the cupboard with its coathangers, are subjected to the same transformations. Only the entrance doors, which "enclose" the space, constitute a fixed and unchanging element. In the shape of two wings, pushed to the side, knocked together out of bare boards, they are what give this space its main emphasis. All the main performers in *Wielopole, Wielopole* enter and exit through them. Behind the doors lies the space which Kantor calls the "antechamber" or "vestibule", a space set aside for the equivocal regions which in some previous period were at the centre of the action. A piece of equipment which plays one of the major parts in the dramatic functions of the room is a large bed, which at first glance looks like a scruffy bit of household furniture, but turns out to be full of mechanical refinements. This is how the room of Kantor's childhood looks when the spectators enter and glimpse, amid these perspectives of wooden space, Kantor himself, flitting through the first, reserved, rows of seats.

When the lights go down, little lamps hanging from fine wires are seen still burning in the space of the room, while Kantor – as usual in his black suit and a black scarf – opens the main doors. At that moment the characters dispose themselves around the stage. Words that were never spoken, but were written as a text prepared for the performance in the role of Kantor himself, lead to a game of who's who:

Here is my grandmother, my
Mother's mother, Katarzyna.
And that's her brother, the
Priest.
Some used to call him uncle.
He will die shortly.
My father sits over there.
The first from the left.
On the reverse of this
photograph he sends his
greetings.
Date: 12 September 1914.
Mother Helka will be here any
minute.
The rest are Uncles and Aunts.
They went the way of all flesh,
somewhere in the world.
Now they are in the room,
imprinted as memories:
Uncle Karol, Uncle Olek,
Auntie Mańka, Auntie Józka.[2]

One might be forgiven for thinking this "keepsake album" roll-call represents nothing more than a young man's recollections, a way of taking stock of the family. This is not the case, since each and every method for disclosing memories has at least two consequences, according to Kantor. Memory makes use of "hired" personages, as Kantor explained. "These are shadowy, mediocre, dubious sorts of creatures, who are waiting to be "hired", like casual charladies." So it comes about that every member of the Kantor family is, in this performance, someone different (cf. Kantor's manifesto "The Employment Agency of the Dear Departed"):

The dodgy-looking bloke over there
kitting himself out like a conscript
is pretending to be my Father.
My Mum is travestied by a blatant street-walker,
and my uncles are common tramps.
The widow of the highly respected town photographer
manfully maintains the repute of the Photo Department
called *Ricordo* but in real life she's just
a disgusting old skivvy
working in the parish charnel-house.
As to the Priest: the less said the better.
His sister is something in catering.
Then there's Uncle Staś, the mournful figure of
A deportee
Backyard Hawker with a Hurdy-Gurdy.[3]

Sequence One, "The Wedding", makes an effort to present the *dramatis personae* among the props. Each one's attempt to be specific about how the room used to look is thwarted. Uncle Karol (Wacław Janicki) makes a futile attempt to exit, in a temper, by the side (moving) door, calling out to Adaś (Lech Stangret) all the while to open the door for him. He is never able to decide whether it is actually a door or not. The Identical Twin Uncle Olek (Lesław Janicki) experiences difficulty with a chair and finds it beyond his powers to fix the position of a (moving) window opposite the side door. The uncles then engage in a full-scale controversy over where exactly a suitcase once lay. Uncle Stasio (Lila Krasicka) returns from the war (and from prison) to the family home, furnished with a violin case which resembles the wing of a wounded bird, and which turns out to be a hurdy-gurdy with a crank handle. The carol *Lullay my Jesus*, in splendidly strangulated musical form, confirms Uncle Stasio's inner conviction of his virtuosity, even though the melody of the carol scarcely reaches the ears of the listeners, and recalls the mangled tune reproduced by an old record.

From the first time the spectator is able to observe the mechanism of the death bed, when the Priest reveals his double role: dying and dead. "In this difficult part", Kantor writes, "I am greatly assisted by his double – a wax dummy". The mechanism of the bed, set in motion by the Photographer's Widow, generates the process which transforms the dead man into the dying. The Photographer's Widow is then forbidden access to the priest's bed by the other widow (Auntie Katarzyna). Armed with a chamber pot, Katarzyna sings songs which are both laments and prayers. She knows when all is said and done that the Photographer's Widow is just a common cleaner from the mortuary. At length the room is enlivened by the Platoon, sounding its horn-calls. Among these recruits, commemorated in their souvenir photograph before leaving for the front, is Kantor's father – Marian. Kantor tries to interpret their dramatic significance in the following terms:

THE PLATOON
They assemble around us
as if in a dream. Menacing and ALIEN.
The alien aspect of the dead appearing in dreams
Photographs of RECRUITS – souvenirs of the dead
Selected and docketed by death,
Infected with the bacillus of death
obscure and violent
which makes them fit to deal out death
to their fellows
themselves perishing under orders
marked down for destruction.[4]

The military drill ends in a posthumous nuptial celebrated against Marian's will by the Priest, who has joined the ranks of the living.

Sequence Two is the consequence of Kantor's return to childhood. As a retrospective view of the "primordial time scale of the individual entity", it

25. The first sequence of *Wielopole, Wielopole*, "The Wedding". Photo: Jacek Barcz

brings about a condensation of time, a sudden foreshortening. The family circle becomes a complex mechanism of actions comprising a system of repetitions. Uncle Karol continues his door-play, Uncle Olek his performance with the chair and the window. The wardrobe, meanwhile, induces in both of them the need to dress up. So when Uncle Olek insists on undressing, and starts hanging up various items of his wardrobe, Uncle Karol begins to dress, loudly naming each item of clothing he puts on. Auntie Mańka (Maria Stangret), with a crucifix and rosary in her hand, declaims verses from the scriptures, while Auntie Józka (Ewa Janicka) goes on as usual unobtrusively trying to draw the family together. Quarrelling among themselves, and plunged in their own peculiar doings, the family find a common language only in the wedding of Helka (Teresa Wełmińska or Ludmiła Ryba) and Marian (Andrzej Wełmiński). The death of the Priest (Stanisław Rychlicki) will be subjected to a certain number of repetitions, as will the mourning ritual of the Grandmother (Jan Książek), intoning Easter hymns with a chamber pot in her hand. The Photographer's Widow (Mira Rychlicka), putting her machine in action, reminds us of the mortality of the cadre of squaddies, since her camera is in fact a machine gun. The repetitive nature of the actions is accompanied by the repetition of the sound, on four tapes: the Easter threnody (recorded in the church in Niedzica) which accompanies the Grandmother's actions; the "prepared" carol which Uncle Staś repeats; and the march, *Grey Infantry*, which is associated with another kind of "rising" . . . the Warsaw Uprising.

A characteristic motif is the endless intertwining of the destinies of Marian and Helka. The failure of communication between the married couple is crowned by an "everyday" story of war: a refined sort of rape of Helka, who has been thrown to the floor. This rape by the gang of soldiers is assimilated to a scriptural image of Golgotha. The rape is also an indication that over there, "beyond the doors", another world is seething – the world of the "Antechamber". In his commentary, Kantor wrote:

> . . . And then there is the place "Behind the Door"
> somewhere at the back and on the edges of the Room.
> a different space
> in a different dimension.
> Where our memories press together
> our liberty breeds
> in this poor place
> somewhere in "a corner"
> "behind the door"
> in some nameless interior of the imagination . . .
> we stand in the doorway saying farewell to our childhood,
> helpless,
> on the threshold of eternity and of death,
> in this small, gloomy space,
> behind this door
> human hell and tempests rage
> the waves are gathering of that flood from which there is no shelter
> in the white weak walls of our Room
> our everyday
> "calendar" time . . .

26. The Uncles, the Priest and his mannequin in *Wielopole, Wielopole*. Photo: Jacek Barcz

A dangerous ferment starts and will shortly take over the room and its inhabitants. In the backyard and antechamber the innocent war games of childhood start up, along with the executions that are copies of various assorted originals; imperceptibly, this game, this rumpus, turns into an all too verisimilar reality. This is how the gang rape of Helka began, and this is how the "court martial" of the Priest begins. In the Third Sequence, Auntie Mańka's premonitions are realised: she has become metamorphosed, in her own person, into the figure of the Intruder in Fascist Uniform, giving orders to the platoon. Military drill (exercises in how to kill) leads to the Way of the Cross for the Priest, and the crucifixion of Adaś. This sequence, repeated over and over again, takes the form of a symbolic death on the cross for the Man of God, who hastens to join the procession, where he bears his own cross. The Lenten clappers, in the hands of the soldiers, proclaim the harvest of death.

The crucifixion of Adaś and commentary by the anxious figure who is the twice-over embodiment of the Priest and his wax dummy, forms an introduction to the sequence "Adaś Goes to War". The main problem in the interpretation of this sequence resides in the metamorphosis of the recruits. Kantor's manifesto reveals:

> In old photographs showing the departure of recruits for the battlefront at various railway stations, we can see smiling faces, even a sort of sexual euphoria, strong young bodies sheathed in dungarees, divorced from their sublimated and intricate cultural, social, and family relations . . . Everything suddenly becomes straightforward, everything is brought down to basics, the whole sclerotic shell of culture falls away, obscene, brutal, cynical . . . At long last it has become "stereotypical".[6]

Conscious of the charms of symbolism, Kantor speaks the language of metaphorically shifting images. An example of this is Adaś's farewell as he goes off to the front, never to return. Through the main door, which has been turned into a goods wagon full of soldiers and mannequins with the help of a vertical screen, naked replicas of soldiers can be seen, images of great expressive power. Soldiers waving their rifles, thrusting the mannequins aside as symbols of birth and death, are seen off by all the members of the stage family. But for Kantor this image is not enough. He adds an element of "disclosure", his own commentary. This takes the form of the Priest's movements, as he throws sand after the departing wagon full of people, from a small mound to the right of the stage, where there is a grave with a cross.

The sequence ends with a Requiem Mass, preparing the way for the final section. The untiring repetition of such elements as the march of the platoon and appearance of Uncle Staś, suggests the destruction of the laboriously constructed set is inevitable. It is hastened on its way by a frenzied march to the tune of *Grey Infantry*[7] and the burial alive of the Priest and the Rabbi. For the finale, Platoon-Desperadoes, together with the Family, construct a table where everyone can sit. When the table has been laid with a white tablecloth, the carol rings out for the last time. It appears that equilibrium has been restored, the image and its verisimilitude conveying the message of the Renaissance humanists. The table has become a contemporary replica of the Last Supper. But this equilibrium cannot last. Its components start to

27. The Priest in *Wielopole, Wielopole*, who will have to bear his own cross. Photo: Jacek Barcz

disintegrate, the impetus weakens, the understanding dies away. Everyone has to leave, including Kantor himself, who is left alone to fold up the tablecloth which traverses the entire width of the stage. When he has finished, the performance is over.

Wielopole, Wielopole is Kantor's most personal play, with an intricately structured emotional component. This production – a step on Kantor's way towards formal perfection – is his most poetic, and is stuffed with multi-layered metaphors. At the same time it is his most didactic intervention; clashing stereotypes, myths, and cultural images play a major part. The combination of formal precision and startling content is peculiarly thrilling. And this thrill is at the root of all true theatre.

Notes

1   See note 3, p. 46.
2   The opening of *Wielopole, Wielopole* in the translation of Hyde and Tchorek.
3   Ibid. Kantor's texts were not sacrosanct and there are a few small differences between the text as translated here by the author, and the Hyde/Tchorek translation of *Wielopole, Wielopole*.
4   Ibid.
5   Ibid.
6   Ibid.
7   Kantor's marvellously effective use of music includes the blatant appropriation of such elements as this *Independence March* from the Polish Legion created by Józef Piłsudski before and during the First World War.

28. The final sequence of *Wielopole, Wielopole*, with the goods wagon full of soldiers and their naked mannequin replicas. Photo: Jacek Barcz.

10

ON THE STATE OF THINGS, THE AVANT-GARDE, INNOVATION, LUCK, TRUTH, AND SUCCESS

(Conversation, June 1981)

KM: The processes of change gaining ground in the political life of the country, striving to transform the social structure of Poland, force us to ask ourselves how art should react in the face of these changes. Is there, in fact, or can there ever be, any simple set of implications concerning the interrelationship of art and life?

TK: You must allow me to answer exclusively on my own account. I take art to be an independent and autonomous entity, in the sense that it does not reflect life directly. Nevertheless, I acknowledge in my own art, and I disseminate, a category of "lived reality" which serves mental and philosophical, as well as formal and artistic, ends. I am convinced an artist will always find himself in some life situation which he has to define clearly to himself as a human being. As far as the Polish situation is concerned, I feel the urge to define my negative attitude to the consumer society of the West, so that we can realise our own special nature and safeguard its potential for shaping a new cultural order.

KM: I am terrified of certain attempts and efforts art may make in its creative endeavours – attempts at fellow-travelling, at illustrating, at affirming – which could be the obverse of the hard-won medal of "committed art" – an obverse as grotesque as it is dangerous.

TK: I have been convinced for many years that art should not be "produced", and I am formally and spiritually committed to that position. Ever since the late fifties and early sixties, I have been locked in debate over all those ways of conceptualising the work of art and its uniqueness, with the state of artistic inspiration, with artistic functions of space, so as to replace them with a notion of reality. But something else concerns me, which is why I feel the urge to recall wartime, which was when I put art, and the work of art, in context for the first time. It was then that I understood (and my production of *The Return of Odysseus* bears this out) that in a "dense" life situation a work of art ceases to have its own significance. So together with my fellow artists in the Underground Theatre, I sought an exit from this situation: one where the art object could be replaced by a real-life object. And from that day to this, I have been possessed by the notion of reality.

In our time, the "real-life" situation is so densely compacted, that it has almost caught up with the reality of art. This is one reason why the pastime of debating aesthetic values in art nowadays seems pretty tedious. A much more important issue than art as such is the cultural dimension of life itself. But the state of this "life-culture" in our country, after years of being ruled by people who on the whole lack any experience or knowledge of culture, is today tragically low. The real task facing everybody who works in the arts or in culture or with the pen, is not the struggle to express a handful of thoughts, but the battle for our culture as a whole, our life-culture. Without that we are lost.

KM: Would you be able to demonstrate how this process manifests itself in relation to the average observer?

TK: Of course. The thesis I have presented is bound up with my own concrete observations. Just look, for example, at Warsaw. That chain of new districts with thousands of identical elements – grey, dirty blocks of flats, erected on the scale of New York skyscrapers – makes a nightmarish impression. A view like that induces sadness, pessimism, conformity in everything a person undertakes.

Obviously, the people who built them could always say their job was to provide as many flats as possible. Very well: but why do these residential areas have to oppress people, why must they weigh them down spiritually with inertia, pessimism, depression, loss of initiative, with all the conditions, in other words, which undermine the harmony of social life? This is not just the view of the aesthete: it is the view of a man who feels the urge to live life to the full.

And one more thing, and I underline it once again: people will say, "Don't weep for the rose when the forest is blazing", chuck out all this

29. Tadeusz Kantor. Photo: Jacek Barcz

untimely and inappropriate aestheticism. In my view, however, this is exactly the right moment to start thinking about beauty.

KM: Your view of "beauty" is rather different from that of our aesthetic theorists . . .

TK: In my view, "the beautiful" is harmony and diversity of form, values which impart happiness to life, and creative energy and mental powers to man. If you think about it in this way, to demand beauty is in no way to contradict the life-needs of ordinary people who – with absolute justification – are asking for flats, and as quickly as possible.

KM: The new districts are depressing in respect of their amenities, too.

TK: What I find most offensive is the material trumpery in the exteriors of these tower blocks, stylised in the shape of some ultra-modern structuring of inter-galactic space. The main entrance, on the other hand, recalls a cattle-shed on a badly-run farm in some village, where cow-dung, slovenliness, and dirt are mixed in equal proportions as if by some law of nature. And nobody does anything about it, because it has affected the mentality of the inhabitants so much.

KM: Who is to blame for this state of things? The inhabitants must take some of the blame for not being able to keep things in order . . .

TK: But only a part of the blame . . . and not the largest part; they are cooped up in these constricting structures. The ones to blame are the presidents, the directors, the bosses, the secretaries, the whole ruling elite who want to pass themselves off as Medicis, but who offer this Maecenas, as he generally likes to call himself, no concrete assistance or support.

KM: Except for a lot of hot air about the "beautiful new districts", which is a stock-in-trade of the propaganda of success.

TK: What's more, they couldn't give a damn, any of them, about their responsibility for beauty in a district that people have to live in. Taste, beauty, culture are purely abstract concepts for the sort of people who decide how our cities should look. There's nothing surprising in the fact that their only goal is to administer culture with the help of specialists chosen by virtue of their sycophancy and conformism. Those pretentious and inflated departments in the Academies of Fine Art and other similar colleges proclaim themselves the "smithies" of industrial forms, urbanism, "applied" architectonics, polychromy. Their spokesmen – professors, readers, senior lecturers – try to do away with "pure" painting and "pure" sculpture so that they can make decisions concerning the beauty of our land without hindrance. This "beauty" we talk so much about bears witness to their ignorance, which is the consequence, in the end, of throwing dust in the eyes of the authorities.

KM: It cries out for concrete interventions aimed specifically at wiping out the anomalies . . .

TK: Art simply has to help itself. I am just as upset by voices in the art world who feel an urge to capitalise on such insights, and thereby renew the social order. These voices can be recognised by their over-simplifications, which once led to the negative phenomenon of socialist realism and its establishment of crude and powerful ties between art and life. As history teaches us, good art always breaks free from any specific political or social programme, while remaining in touch with the deepest layers of social life. That is why the current urge in painting, theatre, sculpture, and literature to reflect or mirror the social order of things, is an exceptionally primitive step to take.

KM: When it comes to art's bonds with social life, you would probably agree with the truth of art mirroring social transformations . . .

TK: Art does do that, but not as part of a schema of the sort signified by the norms of socio-political life. Slogans of a revolutionary ethic become very reactionary where art is concerned.

KM: The slogan, reiterated over and over again, "Art for the masses, art for the workers," highlights the communicative function of language.

TK: But all good art is communicative. I have insisted in Cricot on a concept of "thrill" as the only channel of communication with the spectator. I simply don't reckon with the channel of political information or of social relations. Art is not needed for communicative processes of that sort. What is more, the avant-garde, which I represent, has always battled for the freedom of the human spirit, and has expressed this in our time with real grandiloquence. After 1945, our struggle was sustained in settings and circumstances which were very dangerous for those who supported it. If this is what I have been doing all my life, and if I am doing it today, I really cannot see why I should change in order to find something "innovative". My struggle, then and now, was the struggle of innovation: I struggle for the freedom of man and his personal standpoint. I do that on my own account, but in a different structure, more intricate than that of social life. Secondly, if I consider that the concept of "thrill" is the only medium which can contain the work of art and its spectator, this is just one element in an integrated programme of innovation. And so I stand in opposition to the canons of the academic avant-garde, which asserts its right to "arrange" people's souls.

KM: You have been employing the term "avant-garde". In the light of the manifestos you wrote to accompany your last two achievements, *Dead Class* and *Wielopole, Wielopole*, the word has changed its meaning.

TK: It's worth returning to the problem of the avant-garde, and to how, firstly, the concept took on a special sort of colouring on Polish soil; and secondly, how, thanks to an oversimplified set of critical parameters (in *Dialog*)[1] the understanding of this term was made to seem absurd.

I have frequently drawn attention to the way in which the avant-garde has turned into a mass movement of mediocrities, with people who make their careers out of a few conceptual tricks, diligently concealed behind a screen of bogus theory, people who make a living out of the huge potential for consumption, even – I would say – of cannibalism, artistic omnivorousness, or the formation of a huge market, which confirms the total emptiness of this art.

KM: You emphasised the role of "thrill" as the sole means of getting through to the spectator . . .

TK: Yes, and I would like to underline once more that my art is composed on the basis of a "thrill principle", i.e., I do everything to create a "thrill domain".

KM: Are there no inner contradictions in this?

TK: I know what you have in mind. You're bothered about the contrast between "avant-garde" and "thrill". A lot of avant-gardists have no time for thrills; they think, on the contrary, that thrills are strictly for the crowd, for people who do not understand the essence of art. But there is nothing more untrue than opinions of this kind, especially when they come from representatives of the rank-and-file of the avant-garde. By speaking out against them today, I remain a true . . . avant-gardist. For what, in fact, is the avant-garde? The avant-garde negates convention of all kinds. Today the most widespread convention is the widespread proliferation of avant-garde artists.

KM: You have previously mentioned the simplistic interpretations applied to your expressed opinions, particularly the assertion that you have betrayed the avant-garde, discarded it, verbally abused it, and finally condemned it altogether.

TK: The article in *Dialog*, as well as a few other none-too-responsible accounts, certainly suggested I was against the avant-garde, and that I was spreading abroad the view that the avant-garde was a dead duck.[1] However, I would like to point out that such critics tend to crop up during any expansion of the avant-garde, in the silence before and after a revolutionary storm, evidently delighted to see the end of the avant-garde so that peace can reign at last and the "golden age" of "proper art" begin. Despite the fact that people tried to misinterpret them, my statements were not directed against the avant-garde. I am against the *institutional* avant-garde, because, amazingly enough, opinion has it that such a thing exists in Poland. In fact it isn't avant-garde at all: it is a recycling of a few hazardous borrowings from the great artists. In their day, these items were genuinely disturbing and revolutionary, but now they are just tricks and gimmicks endlessly repeated by thousands of pipsqueaks: they have ceased to be avant-garde.

KM: If we try to sort out all the innovations of your artistic programme . . .

TK: I wouldn't like to leave the idea of truth out. When I speak of truth, I'm not thinking of the weight of moral significance attached to this word, but of the formal consequences of it. Truth, for me, is the counterbalance to the stylisations employed in theatre and literature. So, for example, working on *Wielopole, Wielopole*, I neither had recourse to a ready-made text, nor did I write my own play. I created a structure of representation in the linguistic "strata" so that the raw material of everyday speech remained. Serving initially as the personal element in which the actor moved, this language then became the basic material of the whole production. A year ago I wrote an essay about truth.

KM: Will you recall the main points for us?

TK: I will restrict myself to its two most important propositions. The first is that the artist "creates" more or less within the artistic conventions dominant in a given period. I would cite the example of Wyspiański, who has an impeccable individuality, but whose art lies entirely within the period of the Secession, Art Nouveau, and Modernism. And secondly, individual truth does not lie on the surface of form, but at the bottom of it, emitting waves with a powerful frequency. The opposite of truth is falsehood. We distinguish between private falsehood and public falsehood. Ignorance, low spiritual horizons, and intellectual limitations are permissible in private. But these traits are dangerously false when imposed on others. In my view, such people belong to the same class of offenders as pickpockets. But the law has no such category of crime or punishment. In art, the air is thick with falsehood, attracting social approbation and support by means of a few tricks and gimmicks. Vice-chancellor-artists, professor-artists, dozent-artists, secretary-artists. Just try to imagine the following titles appended to the names of famous artists: President Picasso, Vice-Chancellor Picasso, Professor Picasso, Dozent Picasso.

KM: You have encompassed, through the language of artistic metaphor, all the characteristics that lie in the domain of innovation ...

TK: But that still doesn't constitute an artistic programme. The greatest responsibility of the artist is the possession of an artistic programme, and its realisation. I do not know a single literary or artistic journal in Poland which has its own programme, I have never encountered a theatre, or any other institution, which could give a proper artistic account of itself; the Academy of Fine Art is afflicted with a total lack of ideas. You meet creative artists with a programme, or artists with ideas, very rarely; and when these rare instances arise, we must not only give them proper attention, but take them to our hearts.

KM: Historical examples, I suppose, are the movements from the turn of the century ...

TK: Cubism, Surrealism, Constructivism, *The Points*[2] and Polish Formism.[3]

KM: And today?

TK: I don't know how to answer that question: but it seems to me as if all sorts of writers publish in all sorts of journals. These journals have no programme, they are not aiming to adopt any particular standpoint. This phenomenon is all the more striking because political life in our country is that much "purer" in its radicalism. Different groups are not always trying to win over certain enemies, and are not just indifferent, the way the art world is.

KM: So the moral is that one must work out a programme?

TK: I don't believe in "working out". A programme must come to life spontaneously, as a natural manifestation of the artist.

KM: For many years you have been trying to locate Cricot in some kind of programme ...

TK: Cricot has always had a very precise artistic-conceptual programme: a programme precisely defined at each stage in our investigations.

KM: Two turning points which are particularly crucial in the world reception of your work are *Dead Class* (1975) and *Wielopole, Wielopole* (1980).

TK: Absolutely: those turning points, as you rightly say, are so important that my dream – for the first time, by the way – is to hold on to them. I have managed to find, at such moments, a universality of reception that should stay behind when I have gone. For this reason I have asked the Ministry of Culture to place them under a conservation order, just like the parks set aside for national monuments. I would like them to live in the future through an agency of actors, when I am no longer around. This is placing them *sub specie aeternitatis*, the dream of everyone who takes the theatre arts seriously. It's a dream that says art must survive our life.

KM: Theatre is everywhere considered an ephemeral art, which stays in the mind of the spectator in a kind of legendary state.

TK: The *Cricot 2 Theatre* has been formally constituted to exist "eternally", i.e., longer than any human life. Museums, for example, conserve the imagination of the past in a kind of everlasting life. I believe in this museum-like preservation of the life of a work of art. This is manifested in both Kraków and Florence by two Cricot centres: the Cricotèques.

KM: But over and against this approach to the work of art, and using as evidence your previous opposition to museums, people will insist that a true work of art must be alive.

TK: I did stand out against museums as places, but now I can see that "pickling" a work of art has its own rationale in life terms. I saw, for example, thirty to forty years after the event, a commemorative exhibition of the Bauhaus. The *Triadic Ballet* of Oskar Schlemmer was on film, of course, but in the exhibition it was presented in the form of wax dummies, real-life objects from an exceptionally radical theatre. That was all that remained. But the power of what remained was, and is, so great, that Schlemmer's art has had an influence on all theatrical reformers. The same is true of pictures in museums and galleries. They are not kept and hung in a spirit of unction or sanctimony, like holy relics. They are significant elements of the past, but they are also intended for further development. My personal development, for example, exists in a manipulation of the past.

KM: If I understand correctly what you are saying, this "manipulation of the past" involves a conscious choice, the inevitability of such a choice . . .

TK: Basically, yes . . . which is why I would advise Polish museologists to base their final selection of Polish art on a distinction between works which were important in the development of art, and works needed by the people, society, the individual, for extra-artistic reasons. If even the likes of Malczewski[4] are not subjected to such a selection process – and with Malczewski great art exists alongside kitsch – it will work against the significance of Polish art in the world.

KM: And with that conclusion we should end this exposition which started from a simple proposition: namely that this is the first time in the history of Cricot that you have prepared your next production without rejecting the previous one. On the contrary, you keep going back to it, and setting it alongside your new achievements.

TK: I judge *Dead Class* and *Wielopole, Wielopole* as one, even though they are so different.

30. Advertising for *Où Sont les Neiges d'Antan?* at the Riverside Studios,[5] London, 30 November to 5 December 1982. Photo: Jacek Barcz

Notes

1 Cf.p60, n.3.

2 *Zwrotnica* [switch point – as in railways] – an avant-garde journal that identified with Polish constructivism, published in Kraków by Tadeusz Peiper, the doyen of Polish avant-garde poetry. The name of the journal is explained by a phrase used by Peiper in his introductory article, "Starting Point", published in the first edition in May 1922: "*Zwrotnica* is intended to be a switching-point to the present".

   The first series of *Zwrotnica* consisted of six editions published between May 1922 and October 1923. Apart from Peiper himself, the journal was supported by poets from the Kraków poetic avant-garde movement, including Julian Przyboś, Jan Brzękowski and Jalu Kurek, as well as by the most dynamic theoreticians of the Polish avant-garde movement, Władysław Strzemiński of Vilnius, author of the revolutionary work *Teoria Widzenia* (*Theory of Seeing*) and Mieczysław Szczuka of Warsaw. It also had the cooperation of two avant-garde journals *Blok* and *Praesens*, and the support of the Kraków Formist movement, which later inspired Kantor.

   The second series of *Zwrotnica*, revived in the years 1926–1927, drew attention to avant-garde construction of poetry, and – in art – pointed to the creativity of Kazimierz Malevich, also an idol of the young Kantor.

3 Formism is a Polish version of Constructivism.

4 See note on page xv.

5 The Riverside Studio's poster reads *Where are Last Year's Snows*. This translation was not accepted by Kantor.

11

CRICOTAGE UNDER VILLON'S BANNER

Où Sont les Neiges d'Antan?

1. "Cricotage is a special type of activity which has developed out of the discoveries made by Cricot 2 and the methods of acting realised and put into practice by that theatre." This is how Kantor begins the manifesto which changed at a stroke his definition of "Cricotage".

Cricotage, according to Cricot's creator, is neither a happening, since it rejects audience participation, nor a performance, since it questions the basic premise of "minimal significance".

But equally, Cricotage as a way of making an impact on the spectator is not altogether new for Kantor. It appeared towards the end of 1978, when the triumphant progress of *Dead Class* (1979) had brought its creator acclaim in artistic circles. This bore fruit in three public showings in the last days of January 1979 at Rome's Palazzo delle Esposizioni, at the time of the great exhibition of paintings by Kantor and other artists from the Cricot circle, along with production apparatus and costumes taken from the work of the Kraków group in 1957. Cricotage coincided with this show for half a year before the Florence opening of *Wielopole, Wielopole* (1980).

The French title, *Où Sont les Neiges d'Antan?* (*Where are the Snows of Yesteryear?*)[1] picks up on one of the ballads by the fifteenth century troubadour, criminal and murderer François Villon, recognised as the first modern French poet. Is the title a self-ironising commentary underscoring the theme of transience with a semantic battery of allusions, or is it intimately related to Villon's poetic vision, and the terrifying threat of his realism? Kantor tells us:

Cricotage deals in REALITY
freed from all "fables".
Its fragments, relics and traces
snatched away by the power of IMAGINATION,
flouting every convention and all sound judgement
are interwoven
with just enough resilience
that at any moment they could be
ruptured
and shattered.
This impression
of danger

of endlessly impending
catastrophe
is the basic nexus of Cricotage.

Perhaps the answer can be best elicited from a description of the events of
the play, which offer an interpretation of the points made in this fragment of
a manifesto.

2. The spectator, entering an evenly-lit auditorium, is initially struck by the
layout of the acting area. Two great stands composed of folding seats
designate the centre of action in the form of a narrow quadrilateral. Its limits
are defined by three massive black screens: two recall the wings of a stage,
while the third – a sort of backdrop – is set two or three metres further back.
The longer sides of the quadrilateral define the stage and enclose a figure
posed against the background of black screens: a skeleton on a chair dressed
in a black Jewish gown and black skullcap. As the spectators take up their
places, the Trumpets of Jericho, situated at the end of one of the side screens,
launch into an assembly prophesying the end of the world – another device
from Kantor's collection of machines. On the other side, symmetrically
arranged *vis-à-vis* this device, the eye is caught by a heap of earth with a
shovel in it. A wooden metre measuring-stick has been thrown on to the
earth next to the sand, another significant object, as the action will show. A
skeleton, a trumpet and a heap of earth are the only visual signs to meet the
spectator as he seats himself. They are already familiar to Kantor aficionados:
the skeleton and the heap of earth "appeared" in *Lovelies and Dowdies*
(1973) and *Wielopole, Wielopole* (1980). The Last Trumpet, in a slightly different form, but with a comparable function, appeared in *The Water Hen*
(1969). And there is Kantor himself, patrolling the territory of the previous
performance, lustrating the stage, peering behind the screens to make sure
the actors are not dozing, waiting for the chance to get his Cricotage moving,
because it will have its own discovery to offer him.

3. When, at a sign from Kantor, the lights in the auditorium go down a little,
delimiting the space of the acting area, the spectators can make out against
the black backdrop a white opening from which the end of a rope hangs.
    At the same time, a thin figure appears dressed in white, pulling faces at
the audience. This figure unobtrusively catches hold of the line. When he
pulls it hard, drawing out much of its length, eight people in white leap out
from behind the screen on both sides; their clothes, cut from special paper,
rustle at every step. Thus begins the first sequence of the Cricotage with
rope-tugging in the style of the Volga boatmen. Soon the resistance of matter
shows how illusory these actions have been: the line begins to tug the group
in both directions. Spurred on by inarticulate cries, their efforts are finally
rewarded: the leader of the group triumphantly fastens the end of the line to
a hook next to the skeleton. The line thus divides the space and marks "the
fine line" between life and death. Beyond this line begins a senseless flight
from the skeleton to the screens.

At the end of the group the opponent of the thin man appears: an ambitious fat man, shouting and urging on the deluded people in white who run hither and thither. At the turning-points their flight ends in head-on collision, succeeded by a new burst of energy, and the whole thing starts again. This could have gone on for ever, if one member of the senselessly trotting group had not broken ranks. The metaphor behind this running in the dark is easily decoded. Kantor is quoting from himself: the device of marking out a line with a fixed direction and leading people to their tragic destiny was first used in a celebrated sequence of *Lovelies and Dowdies*, prophesying the death of one of the protagonists.

31. *Where are the Snows of Yesteryear?* The Janicki brothers as the twin Cardinals and Andrzej Wełmiński as the Bridegroom. Photo: Jacek Szmuc

4. The member of the group who broke ranks after coming to his senses – culminating in a general collapse – starts deriding the situation he was a part of not long before. This prompts him to seek contact with the audience. In this way, he tries to emphasise his distance from the group. Looking around, he discovers a tailor's metre rule lying by the heap of earth; he picks it up in delight, because he can turn this ruler into an instrument of torture for the group. Out of malice he measures feet, legs, fingers, chests, noses and other parts of the prostrate bodies, and underlines every measurement with laughter. Each time his laughter is different. When he tries to repeat *ad infinitum* this process of "perverse measurement", absorbed in his own success, he fails to notice how the members of the group are hiding behind the screen, fed up with his scorn. Mocking, and seeking support for his mockery from the audience, the measurer-imposter then beholds the "true" measurer: the person who started the whole thing in the first place and who is now standing beside the skeleton calling to him. The "imposter", scurrying along with the ruler under his arm, pretends not to hear his orders. But the Great Geometer is implacable. In vain the imposter, whom Kantor calls the Village Measurer, chortles and makes eyes at the public. The Geometer orders him to hand over his wooden rule and quietly leave the field of play. So he throws it into the Geometer's outstretched hands and – looking around to see if he is being followed – disappears behind the screens. The Geometer is pleased – he has staked out his territory and extended his boundary, making use of these people, and now he has hold of the indispensable tool of his trade. The ceremony of true measuring commences: the third sequence

32. The first sequence of the Cricotage begins with tugging on the rope in the style of the Volga boatmen. Photo: Jacek Szmuc

begins, and is just as strenuous as the previous two. The Geometer busily measures the rope and like an old tailor, eggs himself on with murmurs of self-congratulation. He does it so skilfully that halfway through he is able to speed up. The accelerated actions are accompanied by louder and louder chanting of the numbers, until he is babbling and panting. In the ensuing silence all you can hear is a spitting noise – a sign of complete relaxation after a job well done. The line between Life and Death has been drawn definitively.

5. Hurling abuse at the audience, who have been diverted by the preceding sketches, the Geometer falls into his own trap. The line leads him to the skeleton. Some power orders him to exchange his white, rustling attire for

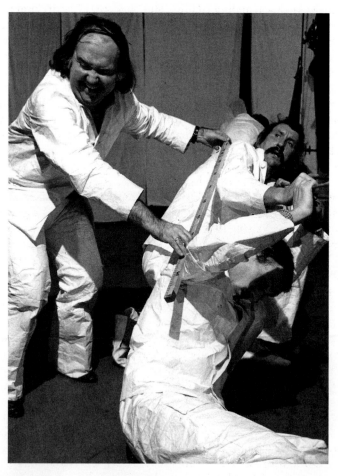

33. The Village Measurer (Krzysztof Miklaszewski) tries to repeat *ad infinitum* the process of "perverse measurement" on his colleagues (Roman Siwulak and Wacław Janicki). Photo: Jacek Szmuc

the gown that garbs the skeleton. As is always the case with Kantor, the simple action of dressing and undressing takes on ritual significance. This happens thanks to the unfolding of the action in the form of tiny episodes of "mini-movements". The scene of simultaneous dressing and undressing by the two Uncles in *Wielopole, Wielopole* has its descendant in *Where are the Snows of Yesteryear?* The Geometer begins dressing, starting from one sleeve of the Hassidic gown, he ends with the skullcap and sidelocks which he takes from the skeleton's skull. The transformation is complete. Enter the Jewish Patriarch and the Jewish Student, a miniature version of the Geometer, and here ends the first part of the performance, although the entire action has lasted scarcely twelve minutes.

6. The second part consists of three sketches, concluding in a group scene of lamentation, calling to mind the burning of the Warsaw ghetto.

It all starts with a sequence of clowning reminiscent of Chaplin. A jovial sort of chap, with a parting down the middle of his head, a paunchy individual, sets off on a walk. On his back a package wriggles, evidently hampering the freedom of his movements. Our "Gentleman" at first cannot identify the luggage he has previously picked up, grown ashamed of and hidden behind his back, and in time forgotten. The package weighs him down, but he is unable to disencumber himself of it. When he finally detaches the package from his body, the problem remains of how to deal with its unravelling. He tries unsuccessfully to wrap it up again, which inspires the Twins in white outfits to offer their idiotic "instructions". The Twins – members of the group pulling the rope – accompany him, and depending on how successful his packing is, they mimic him in various styles with comments of "good" or "bad". This performance is cut short by the impatience of the Twins, egged on by Kantor, who is having great fun with his audience. As the Twins attempt to oust the Gentleman from the field of action, it seems as if a moment of peace will follow. But nothing of the kind. Scarcely has the nonsense with the parcel come to an end, when the Lover of the Press appears. His pockets stuffed with papers, he reads them with aversion, distaste, pleasure, and sometimes anger. During the famed walk along the lines of life and death, this "pressomaniac" throws to the floor his "wretched papers". The Twins give him unexpected backing: they gather up the newspapers in his wake, shout out their names, pass comment on the contents of the articles in every possible variant of "oh!" and "ah!", smack their lips, and at the same time express a certain distance and disapproval with a derisive raspberry. When the "reader", too, is sent packing, the next trio of people in white appears. One of them grabs the shovel, gathers a quantity of earth and hurries blindly off with it. The rest follow, giving him furtive, derisive looks. The trio skating along the hall holds the attention of the spectators for a while. But suddenly on the other side of the rope another trio is in competition: a Streetwalker in a bridal veil is vamping the Twins, who are wearing red Cardinal mitres. Fascinated by her, the Twins try to maintain contact at any price. The girl, however, cannot tell them apart – and a real comedy of errors ensues. After a while there is a gradual change of

34. The Bridegroom (Andrzej Wełmiński), the dead Bride (Teresa Wełmińska) and the Cardinals (Lesław and Wacław Janicki) in *Where are the Snows of Yesteryear?*

mood: people with buckets intervene. Totally robotic, they keep up their movements and pour water from bucket to bucket, reminding the Rabbi of wartime disasters. The Rabbi begins to run like a madman around the Trumpets of Jericho with his pupil, intoning at intervals the words of the hymn of the ghetto, "Our town is burning." This tragic song in nine languages has a terrifying ring as it is howled out against the rhythm of those movements, which are repeated without respite. The demonic atmosphere of the scene is reinforced by the arrival of the repulsive figure whom Kantor refers to as The Man We Know Well. Dressed in high boots and an army cape "with a familiar cut", this individual does his triumphal round of a space already tainted by pain, suffering and dread.

Kantor makes use here of two parallel means of expression: everyday elements based on primary factors, and simultaneous actions bound together in one instant, which disperse the attention of the spectators. This recalls the methods of winning over the audience, then distancing them, employed in *The Water Hen* and *Lovelies and Dowdies*. Several meaningful words, supported by the music, subtly introduce motifs which will burst out in the finale. Alongside the colours white and black Kantor has introduced with great finesse the colour red, as if to prepare the spectator for a shock.

7. The climax of *Where are the Snows of Yesteryear?* is prepared with great exactitude. First comes the ritual of dressing the Bridegroom, more ceremonious than the business with the Geometer. The Bridegroom has to cope somehow with the complicated material of his outfit (braces and bracelets, pins, eyelets etc) and then prepare everything necessary to receive the Bride, whom the spectators have recognised in the course of the hanky-panky with the Twins. When it turns out that the Bride is dead, the wedding turns into a funeral. The Bridegroom pulls the dead Bride along on a mattress and starts the sounding of the Trumpet of Jericho by the two Jews. The Rabbi and the little Jewish Student look after the Trumpet of Jericho. The Rabbi works the machinery, showing off his skills as he slowly pushes the Trumpet forward. The little one runs around him, clutching his head. The Trumpet is then drowned out by the first bars of an Argentine tango. The Twins come in as Cardinals, wearing black surplices and dancing the Argentine tango with variations. In the midst of it all is Kantor, who hums along with the tune, beats out the rhythm, and tries to control the synchronised movement and

35. People with buckets are conducted by Kantor in the sequence "Our town is burning" from *Where are the Snows of Yesteryear?* (from the left: Kantor, Stanisław Rychlicki, Krzysztof Miklaszewski, Roman Siwulak, Zbigniew Gostomski). Photo: Jacek Barcz

sound. This is the most fascinating scene, in which the Cricot method comes to fruition. After a while the participants slip away. Only the dead Girl remains in her bridal dress and veil. Then the people in white run in again, and make a bridegroom's shroud out of their startlingly white paper clothes, which rustle loudly. But the shroud falls to the floor and the paper is dragged along to the rhythm of the tango. Almost imperceptibly the rhythm changes: the tango gives way to a heavy military tread which drowns out everything. The shroud falls on the woman, they all fall to their knees, and the Man We Know Well enters the acting area, marching across the stage. The Street People, as Kantor calls the people in white, then withdraw.

36. The Rabbi (Zbigniew Gostomski) and the little Jewish Student (Dominika Michalczuk) look after the Trumpet of Jericho. Photo: Jacek Barcz

8. The audience's impression of the show is intensified by the repetition of events from the prologue. During the incursions of The Man We Know Well, who has wandered from *Where are the Snows of Yesteryear?* into *Wielopole, Wielopole* the taut line slackens: the line of life and death. Kantor seizes the line, which begins to tug him towards the screen it originally came from. The military personage carries on marching, making for the exit, and Kantor distractedly follows the line. When the marching has quietened down, the end of the line is already hanging in the white hole of the screen, and Kantor is no longer on stage. He has vanished with the rest of them. The circle of events has drawn to a close. The action is finished, but the words of Kantor's manifesto ring on in our ears:

> Despite its clear reference to life
> experiences, it does not in the least
> fulfil our expectations of a development
> founded upon the logic of life. It would be
> an unforgivable simplification
> to try to interpret it via these meanings.

12

THE THEATRE IS ART, FIRST AND FOREMOST

(Conversation, November 1983)

KM: The triumphant advance of Cricot 2 on the stages of every continent in the last eight years has been greeted in Poland with scepticism. In so-called professional circles, the word has spread that your art is not theatre. And your group, which has been performing for twenty years, has been denied the designation of "theatre company".

TK: Cricot 2 is theatre beyond any shadow of a doubt, but the atypical structure of the group makes it hard to classify according to generally accepted conventions. This arises from the programme adopted with specific objectives when the group was founded in 1955. The programme and its ideas have been tirelessly implemented and revised to the present day, and continue to be developed.

KM: So it was the initial state of affairs that was decisive . . .

TK: It was the new state of affairs in the arts and the new ideas taken on board by the groups of artists – actors, painters, poets, musicians – who sought new territories to explore their respective disciplines. These ideas elevated the notion of imagination as the most important component of art; which was altogether shocking in the wake of Socialist Realism. These ideas were ideally suited to the theatre, and allowed particular groups to give communal expression to certain powerful laws of *transformation* in performance; they developed the action and ensuing situations by means of remote associations, gave a new significance to costume and decor and created new relations between the stage and the spectator. But it was the sharply defined new content which determined the revolutionary form of the procedures, and this raised the artistic temperature and strengthened expressive powers, establishing new relations between the literary element and the autonomous element of theatre per se. In a word, a rejection of the customs which had dominated the theatre up to that time.

KM: Ideas of this kind, undermining the schemas shaping theatrical performances in conventional theatre, formed the basis of the concept of autonomous theatre.

TK: Yes, but at the time when the group was formed, it wasn't just a question of theatre. We formed Cricot 2 in the belief that the power of establishing a theatre, and expressing its essence, depended upon making a break with the function of reproducing or displaying works

of literature. It also depended upon the discovery of one's own material and energy, and one's own means of expression, by means of
forming strong links with contemporary art *in total* and its ideas and
tendencies. I am quite sure this is how all theatre groups came about, as
well as the revolutionary cabarets devised by great artists.

KM: You diverted your energy away from "existing theatre art", which you
call "a nexus existing beyond the limits of the theatre, on the literary
plane", and shocked the professionals, because in its 28 years of existence Cricot 2 has presented no more than ten new productions.

TK: But they are not "new productions". We focus less on the "presentation" of a theatrical work of art than on the shaping of our own
material and the structure of our theatre, so that working in a new situation and a new aesthetic, concepts like "première" and "repertoire"
have lost their meaning. As far as these "results" of theatre work are
concerned, we should speak rather about the different "stages" which
have been defined by these results.

KM: Can you describe your work on creating a new piece?

TK: I search with my group for a new form and content of expression,
focusing always on the imperative of spontaneity, the sine qua non of
all creative work. At first this takes only the most shadowy of forms,
more like the negation of the status quo or a premonition. This is slow
work, leading to ever more explicit situations, bringing to consciousness new content, the recognition and mastery of new laws and
principles of action. All this is work in its own right, unrelated to any
kind of theatre art. And only when this independent "scenic" dimension is strong enough and has bonded with other structures do we
introduce the text.

KM: The text of a play?

TK: Generally the text of a play. And generally – a play by Witkacy. I used
him in *The Cuttlefish, The Country House, The Madman and the
Nun, The Water Hen, Lovelies and Dowdies, Tumour Brainard* – I
mean in *Dead Class*, which came out of Witkacy's play.

KM: You were "playing with Witkacy" – as you pointed out after the première of *Dead Class*. On each occasion, the text was steered by a
different key idea – in the Happening Theatre it was *The Water Hen*, in
the Impossible Theatre *Lovelies and Dowdies* and in the Theatre of
Death *Dead Class*.

TK: The autonomous theatre, with origins in the Underground Theatre
and its premières of *Balladyna* and *The Return of Odysseus*, allowed us
to realise our ideas about theatre per se, its content and form, as a portrait of its age.

KM: The last stage of Cricot 2's tireless international tour throws up the
problem of a piece's "run". *Dead Class*, for example, has played more
than one thousand one hundred times in eight years!

TK: Up to the time of *Dead Class*, the "run" business was taken account of
by the gradual satiation of the audience and simultaneous exhaustion of
the means of expression, which in its turn produced a natural demand

for new territories to explore. *Dead Class* and its numerous tours, then the Cricotage *Where are the Snows of Yesteryear?*, and our latest statement, *Wielopole, Wielopole* (produced in Florence), changed the structure of our activities to a certain extent: there were longer intervals between the different stages of our research, and the creative process was supplemented by a demonstration of what had already been shown.

KM: One might say, then, that the structure of Cricot 2 had grown closer to that of professional theatre, for which the "run" is fundamentally more important than the actual creative process.

TK: Indeed, at first glance you might get the impression that the number of productions and frequency of their public performances resembled the kind of "run" practised by professional theatre. But it would be unthinkable for Cricot to put on a lengthy series of performances in one place. Cricot became a touring theatre, which came absolutely naturally to the group. The idea of the touring theatre – a rather over-used term of late – is bound up with theatre in general, or, perhaps, a particular kind of theatre. Not every theatre can be a travelling theatre, but the dynamics of the travelling theatre are by no means the consequence of travelling, as such. It is the structure of the ensemble which gives rise to it being designated in this way.

There is a caricature version of the touring theatre in the form of the "theatre-on-an-excursion", spreading the home-grown product and "disseminating by force".

The dissemination of culture and art is a complex business. I am deeply convinced that in this day and age, the inventor has no obligation to spread his invention far and wide. This is the business of the mass media; it is their job to present new discoveries – including the artist's discoveries – to the world, to interpret them, to disseminate them. When conventional theatre mechanically accommodates its productions to a box stage and pretends to be a "travelling theatre", it becomes pretentious and ridiculous.

KM: Travelling theatre, peripheral theatre, theatre despised and slighted . . .

TK: Precisely how things are with Cricot. All our procedures go back to the fairground sideshow,[1] largely forgotten for over half a century and eclipsed by transient ideas such as the constructivist revolution, surrealist interventions, abstractionist metaphysics, happenings, environments, open theatre, conceptual theatre, antitheatre, great battles, hopes, and illusions as well as great defeats, disillusionments, and pseudoscientific *dégringolades*. In successive periods I signalled different "stages" and "milestones", like the signposts of wayside halts: *Théâtre Informel, Zero Theatre, Impossible Theatre, Theatre of a Poor Reality, Theatre-on-the-Road, Theatre of Death*. It was always at heart the same thing: a fairground sideshow, using various names to protect it against official and academic standardisation. These names also described the long periods in which I negotiated the difficulties that led me always towards the Unknown and the Impossible.

KM: Vakhtangov, recalling Blok's play *The Showman's Booth*, which was produced three times by Meyerhold, was also fascinated (just like you) by the charm of the "low-grade decorations and costumes, the pathos of sad pierrots and prestidigitators, hiding their wrinkles and defeats and tragic human condition under the masks of formality and gestures of nobility."

TK: I wrote in my manifesto: "There is one familiar moment in all theatre when a dangerous and poisonous charm is at work, when they dim the lights and the audience leaves the auditorium – everything on stage turns grey, distant perspectives turn into everyday poster colours, costumes and props are cast aside, and everything that seemed so splendid and radiant now parades its pathetic tawdriness and sham; feelings and gestures die, though a moment ago they were so vibrant and passionate, and so applause-worthy."

I asked the question with *that* image before my eyes: was it merely fiction?

KM: Your return to the showman's booth, which was bound up with your work on *Wielopole, Wielopole*, is indicative of one of the influences on the Cricot group. This was the travelling theatre, in the special sense of the showman's booth at the Shrovetide Fair.

TK: That, too, has a fundamental significance in the reception of Cricot. After passing through dozens of stages and battles, I can see the path I have quite clearly signposted and I can see why I so stubbornly refused institutional and official status and support. Or rather why my theatre and I were so stubbornly denied the privileges and social position which that path should have commanded. It was always a sort of fairground sideshow.

KM: The idea of the journey is a powerful one in your art.

TK: The idea of the journey – and perhaps theatre critics do not know what art critics ought to know – often appeared in my writings as well as in my art. I made a mass of costumes expressing the idea of the journey, organised several happenings expressing this idea, and painted about two hundred pictures full of "journey" elements. The journey motif was far from being a programmatic statement relating to my private inclinations, and what's more, I really don't like travelling! It arises, rather, from a sort of philosophical position: human life as a journey, art as a journey, all sorts of places connected with journeying. The unknown, the unexpected, the strenuous, risk – the components of journeying, travelling, making a pilgrimage. Focusing long since on the topic of the journey, I have begun to talk, in the last few years, about travelling theatre.

KM: Let us go back, then, to the structural changes in Cricot 2 which are connected with travelling. The Cricot theatre receives invitations from pretty well everywhere in the world.

TK: This places certain obligations on me, while reinforcing my conviction that it is Cricot's lot to travel. For centuries, artists from every country travelled eagerly around the world. Not in comfort, as we do today, but on foot or by carriage, hungry and cold, over mountain and sea. Why do they travel? The first motive is the ambition to disseminate their ideas, the urge to express them, because this is the rationale of art. The second is curiosity, curiosity about the world, the whole world. And one more reason, maybe the most important: the unconscious desire to look at one's birthplace from a distance, to take a broad view of it. This is a secret particular place coded in the genes of each of us. Not one's native land, one's birthplace. A place whose main characteristic is that you leave it in order to return in the end. This return is extremely important and fundamental. Art is quite simply the endeavour to get back to that place.

KM: Poles can be pretty intolerant of "world" artists, dubbing them carpet-baggers . . .

TK: This odd phenomenon is as natural as the migration of birds, and should not be reduced simply to the artist who is "old hat" in his own country, the "no man is a prophet in his own land" scenario, or even the artist who is looking for a new lease of life, some higher cultural form beyond the parochialism of his own backyard. Those are common situations and everyday realities; but there is something more fundamental at stake. I have no wish to bore you with the story of my own homecoming, so I simply do not talk about my homesickness for my native land, but rather nostalgia for my childhood. Homesickness and nostalgia are disturbing intimations of some sort of absence, which raises the creative temperature.

KM: We have touched here upon a very sensitive issue, which is fundamental to understanding your way of thinking about your art. Your last two shows, *Dead Class* and *Wielopole, Wielopole*, famous everywhere in the world, took on a form which made them universally intelligible – whether to Australians, the Japanese, Mexicans, or people of the Mediterranean. At the same time, however, they remained purely Polish, with roots deep in Polish traditions. Both productions are a return to "childhood, our birthplace – our most proximate homeland".

TK: This answer contains a question: is Shakespeare less rooted in the cultural traditions of his country than Mickiewicz or Wyspiański? Why is nationalism, together with a lack of universal scope for action, so unremittingly ascribed to our Romantic writers? Who is to blame for this? Certainly not Mickiewicz or Wyspiański. I am convinced that *Forefather's Eve* and *Liberation* should be intelligible to the whole world. And if so, why aren't they?

KM: We have entered, so to speak, the "eye of the storm" of the national culture . . .

TK: If only you knew! There are many different viewpoints concerning the problem of national art and theatre, many inaccurate judgements passed in the name of national culture, judgements which take hold only too easily. Polish art cannot be properly judged in terms of whether certain works are "more" or "less" national. Such procedures have often ended with the extermination of works judged as "anti-national". We know of several sad epilogues[2] to this historical process.

KM: What, then, does the significance of national art depend upon?

TK: A national art only begins to matter when it manages to cross its national frontiers. If this does not happen it is just parochial. Obviously this is difficult: perhaps more difficult than transforming society itself. The life of art and culture is born in the deepest levels of human activity. It refuses to be subjected to superficial or crude manipulation. And there is something else, too, which we might call "race memory". It is contained as much in works as in deeds. Not to be too emotive, I would say it also exists in our childhood. And there is something else, which I would call the "life" of art. Life is endless growth. Growth is the permanent march of change, discarding worn-out conventions which die off and ruin the economy of life. It is the discovery of new folk expression, new consciousness. This phenomenon has existed for centuries, but in our time it has acquired the designation "avant-garde", and despite the vulgarisation of this term by our commodity culture, it does matter that we should not discard the concept. Distrust of the term "avant-garde" may even lead to a simple regression to obscurantism. Discriminating between these two entities is perhaps the very condition of art's existence: national and universal.

KM: To conclude this discussion of the wandering lifestyle of Cricot, I want to ask how your recent experiences have shaped this lifestyle?

TK: It is my ambition to leave an artistic trace in other countries, I try to exert an influence on the development of their art. Something of the sort happened in the course of our eight-month stay in Florence. The press was united in its evaluation of our cultural influence.

KM: When we speak of the "roots" of Cricot theatre, we are foregrounding the idea of the avant-garde, which you speak of constantly. The text about a sort of "general levy" of the avant-garde in your *Theatre of Death* manifesto made a huge impact.

TK: That text took shape in 1973. It was reprinted two years later to accompany the production of *Dead Class*. Here is a fragment of it:

> Leaders, counsellors, signboards, signposts, signals, centres, Art Combines, guarantee the smooth functioning of creative art. We are witnesses to a GENERAL LEVY of the artists – commandos, street combatants, "interventionist" artists, "postmen" artists, epistemological peddlers, street jugglers, managers of Bureaux and Agencies. The traffic on this highway (officially adopted), which threatens to inundate us with scribblers, and with virtually meaningless performances, grows with every day that passes. We must get off it as fast as possible.[3]

KM: This manifesto was received by many zealous opponents of the avant-garde as grist to their mill. The debate about the end – or, as they said, the "death" – of the avant-garde bore witness to an innate artistic conservatism. Some of them could not conceal their pleasure that you – one of the most zealous spokesmen of the avant-garde movement – had abandoned a position you no longer respected.

TK: I do not believe at all that the concept of the avant-garde has been devalued. What is more, I am more and more convinced that an avant-garde position should by no means be limited to one single – mainly early – period of work. We all know the avant-garde is considered to be something youthful, an explosive phase in the life of a generation, after which everything dies down and the artist can get on with more "serious" thoughts creating something more "solid"; as though the avant-garde period is a sort of preparation or rehearsal. The more liberal view is that this "explosion" is necessary to create great or eternal works of art.

KM: The avant-garde has found itself in a strange position, somewhere between the conservative Scylla and pseudo-avant-garde Charybdis.

TK: Some people have been defending the pre-war avant-garde, which became increasingly more academic after the war ended. Others, the representatives of the "great avant-garde levy", are busy converting art's breakthroughs into its small change.

The best evidence of this is the happening, some elements of which put in an appearance from time to time on Polish stages. The happening, such a crucial part of the avant-garde, turned into an easy source of theatrical effects and gimmicks for directors who knew nothing of its genesis and functions.

More or less camouflaged urges towards a "whole" and "integrated" art that would be fit to represent our times in a strong and serious fashion keep making their appearance. Expectations of this kind are full of naivety and over-simplification. They arise from the superficial conviction that our era consists of glaring contrasts, contradictions, tumultuous conflicts – remote from any wished-for "wholeness" – that it is historically anomalous, bearing the stigmata of decadence and cultural twilight. The fact is that "wholeness" cannot be perceptible or recognizable to us in the modern age. Only time provides it when we are gone. This process, enacted by time, does not help us at all.

KM: Where the avant-garde is concerned, terms like "workshop", "experiment", "search", and "laboratory" are used a great deal.

TK: All those concepts bear the familiar stigmata of academicism. They make their appearance and take on their "significance" at the very moment when ideas ossify. From the outset, they are linked to a particular constriction of horizons and relationships, the total integration of art and life, the search for support and assistance in canonical writings, sectarian prescriptive formulae, and the atrophy of invention and imagination.

In art, a new idea is always synonymous with the perfection of the means of its expression. This is the "wonderful" in authentic creation, when revelation coincides with perfection. To draw attention to the "search" and "experimental" – terms borrowed from the domain of science – is a convenient camouflage where art is concerned, lending a phoney sort of status. Creative art is not an attempt, it is a commitment, a discovery. (In my attack on the pseudo-avant-garde I repeated Marcel Duchamp's definition of art's decisiveness.) "Discoveries" in art are made in completely unpredictable circumstances, often ludicrous or scandalous. What is more, it happens at the speed of light. A "discovery", or rather the creation of a "new expressiveness", can exist only on a plane where a large number of frequently contradictory ideas have been erased, at the high temperature of the immediate present. It also exists – not in the poky backyard of professionalism – but in the annexation of "alien" territory via the transgression of professional boundaries, via the betrayal of what has been considered up to now the kernel, the quintessential element, in any given discipline.

KM: Cricot is not an institutional theatre: its internal workings depend upon the "social contract" of its members, people eager to work with you, and who would not work in any other theatre. Why so?

TK: What brought them was their desire to collaborate on my idea of the artistic journey, and their distrust of officialdom. This distrust is fully justified, although it can also lead them to sanction institutions and authorities which often turn out to be false. Officialdom has to rely upon the apparatus of authority, and that is its nature. And its weakness. Officialdom cannot allow itself to approve of any developments which threaten it, or which in the language of officialdom are discreetly labelled "controversial". Officialdom has to rely upon the unshakeable seriousness and dignity of its representatives: directors, presidents, secretaries, dozents, and professors. Sustained by seriousness, the apparatus of officialdom functions splendidly, but in art this produces terrible consequences. There are official theatres, official galleries, official painters, official critics: and the worst are official works of art. There are even official dissidents, who come out with their dissident proclamations, but remain in their art uncommitted and conformist.

KM: Professionals and critics deny members of Cricot the definition of "actor".

TK: Whatever anyone has said or written on this subject, the actors of Cricot exist and will go on existing. They have been "formed", like my theatre, without any kind of blueprint. There is a paradox in the fact that the collapse of nineteenth century bourgeois morality enabled the actor to win a proper social status. Later, the revolution of the twenties further raised the status of the actor into a functionary of avant-garde culture. But as industrial and technical civilisation grew, art lost its avant-garde and dynamic position, and the actor turned into a functionary of theatre as an institution. The rights that had been won changed inexorably into bonds, tying him to bourgeois society which bases its existence and philosophy upon an extreme pragmatism, the cult of utility and automation, thus contradicting the upheavals of art's intervention. Assimilation by this society disarmed and domesticated the actor in his capacity as an artist. The powers of resistance which had been so important to him were taken away, and he was reduced to obedience to the laws of a society of production and consumption, and a loss of independence. Positioning him *outside* society, this independence would have allowed him to influence it. Thus one of the elements of the last reform of the theatre had to be a battle for a new actor, taking into account the deep foundations of his art.

KM: Referring to your manifesto, *The Condition of the Actor*, which begins with the words, "The actor is the naked aspect of man placed on public show", one critic discusses the "entropic acting" of these "lovers of the heavy landing", the "gathered treasure" that comes from "the fascination of the ur-avant-garde, whose model was the clown."

TK: From this review of *Dead Class* there resounds a critical voice of the "how things were" kind, a voice fundamentally hostile to the avant-garde. It's curious that people of this type never cast their eye over conventional academic art: *that's* how things were.

KM: The fascination of the circus is exceptionally important in the genealogy of Cricot. It is contained in the name. Cricot is an anagram of "to cyrk" ("it's a circus"), made at the time of the first Cricot, when Józef Jarema was in charge: he was a passionate connoisseur of the circus.

TK: Most certainly. But let us stick to the impressionistic, but typical, view expressed by our critic. For the conservatives in our profession, the clown has nothing in common with the actor. The circus, like the waxworks show, always existed on the periphery of institutional culture. Dedicated to the *gestus* of the populace, they were rejected by the bourgeois mentality. And this despised gestus has remained in our art and our society until today. The spirit of the circus is embodied in the canvas of the great Polish painter Maria Jaremianka,[4] Józef's sister. Not to mention the post-war pictures by Picasso, where circus games with human anatomy is the outcome of a diabolical conjuring trick. This spirit of the circus is strong in Beckett's work. Also Witkacy and Gombrowicz. The great "musical ringmaster", the greatest musical authority of the twentieth century, Eric Satie, writes: "Let us not forget our obligation to the circus and to those geniuses, the Fratellini Brothers from the Cirque d'Hiver. Our newest and most radical ideas and conceptions of art derive from the circus. This is where the spirit of innovation resides." So let us leave in peace our critic, whose little learning leaves a lot unlearned.

KM: It is worth adding that the genealogy of the circus spirit is not just a matter of circus props or even performing in the ring.

TK: The initiator of Cricot is actually a devotee of "intellectual" clowning. Where you have art with a capital "A", the problem is that much greater. Art is influenced in an unparalleled degree by the sphere of the imagination and "impossibility", which are neither historical nor "real-life" formations, but link up rather with the deep layers of the unconscious and human existence. Theatre is art above all. If its development is close to our heart, we cannot shut ourselves away in a purely professional enclave. We must go "beyond" theatre so as to make contact with art as a whole, with the general current of thought.

KM: You are about to embark on yet another Polish tour. *Wielopole, Wielopole*, after being shown in Warsaw and Kraków, will go off to its birthplace – Wielopole. The tour has been preceded by massive public interest. For years now there have been thousands of spectators at

37. Kantor during rehearsal of *Let the Artists Die!* with Jan Książek.
Photo: Wojciech Kryński

Cricot productions. Do you have positive feelings about this ever-increasing dissemination of your ideas?

TK: I do have positive feelings, I give my consent to all the journeys and structural changes they involve. Moreover, it seems to me that our productions are filling a gap which young people nowadays are trying to put into words, and upon which the future of art will depend. Going back to my native Wielopole will be a great experience for me.

Notes

1 When Kantor talks of the "showman's booth" (or circus), he is recalling the folk theatre of the turn of the century which flourished (especially) in Russia, and left its mark on modernist theatre and poetry. Two much-cited instances are Stravinsky's *Petrushka* and Blok's *Balaganshchik* (hereafter *The Showman's Booth*).

2 Kantor is referring to examples of Polish nationalism which appear in critical appraisals of works of art and theatrical dramas. For the Poles, deprived of their freedom for two centuries, promotion of national pride was an essential aspect of art. Kantor is averse to basing judgement on this. He feels that patriotism must not be mistaken for artistic merit. In post-partition Poland, it was fashionable for art critics to pay homage at the altar of art which depicted battles and scenes of national martyrdom. Kantor's comment on the paintings of the famous Kossak family of Kraków is well-known. With due artistic honesty, he accused them of producing total "kitsch". Similarly, a great exhibition of the works of the Polish symbolist painter, Jacek Malczewski, which was being shown worldwide, did not achieve its desired effect. The Poles had again made the mistake of emphasising the nationalist vein of Malczewski's work, rather than his artistic mastery.

3 From Kantor's *Theatre of Death Manifesto*, published in Warsaw, November 1975.

4 See note 4, p. 2.

13

LET THE ARTISTS DIE!

(Notes from the year 1985)

The questions people started asking in connection with Kantor's next venture, when he said he was starting on a new production, are reminiscent of those found in the sporting press on the future attainments of some famous outstanding sportsman. Will he succeed yet again? Can Kantor sustain his almost ten-year domination of world theatre? Will he once again manage to grab everyone by the ears and affect them as powerfully as he did in *Dead Class* or *Wielopole, Wielopole*?

As an artist with a highly developed sense of his responsibilities, Kantor felt the burden of questions of this kind, but at the same time he did not want to avoid the risks implicit in his new rehearsals. These began with the title, and the stories bound up with it.

KM: The title of your latest work, is full of bitter irony and exemplifies society's attitude to the artist: there is also a story behind it . . .

TK: It all began with a *vernissage* in Paris, at the Galerie de France, with which I have had longstanding and rewarding links. The exhibition was a great success. After it had opened with a party organised by the gallery owner, Catherine Thieck, a lot of people gathered from all over Europe: one of them was Dr Karl Gerhard Schmidt . . .

KM: The Nüremberg banker who sometimes came to Kraków?

TK: We would invite him to come in exchange for the hospitality he had shown me and the Cricot 2 theatre at the time of our two visits to Nüremberg. Schmidt, who comes from a banking family, brought with him his lifelong passion for art.

KM: His Nüremberg gallery is famous all over Europe, not least because of its location . . .

TK: It's in his bank.

KM: One of the banks forming part of his Franconian "Schmidt Bank" chain.

TK: Schmidt is a great lover, connoisseur, and benefactor of contemporary art, following in his father's footsteps as a sponsor of the Wagner festival in Bayreuth. Casting my mind back to that evening more than three years ago, I recall it was Schmidt who introduced the subject of a new production. He was very keen to know what I was working on, and even keener to try out his proposal . . .

KM: For you?

TK: For me and for the theatre . . . I knew he wanted to tell me something terribly important, but being the cultured, discreet sort of chap he is, he was waiting for the right opportunity. And so it happened that when I began dreaming up my first narratives about the production I was planning, Schmidt asked whether I would insert some "Nüremberg" elements . . .

KM: Did this request surprise you?

TK: I was a bit startled – all I could say was "Nüremberg"? But then I sort of shouted the next word: "The nail!"

KM: I remember your fascination with the nail that transfixed Wit Stwosz's cheek. Like the knife in the Kraków Cloth Hall, symbolising the fratricidal conflict of the builders of the towers of St Mary's Church, it terrifies the tourists.

TK: The difference is that while the story of the knife the builder used to kill his more gifted brother merges into fairy tale, the story of Stwosz, one of the most interesting creative artists of his time, seems an excellent illustration of the conflict between the artist and society. I would even go so far as to say that the nail, as far as I'm concerned, has turned into a symbol which is pretty unambiguous: artists are victims of society.[1]

KM: How did Dr Schmidt respond to your outburst?

TK: He immediately cottoned on to the fact that I was referring to Stwosz and the tragic period when he lived and worked in Nüremberg.

KM: Stwosz's name would have been on everyone's lips as the 450th anniversary of his death was coming up, a day that was significant both for Kraków and for Nüremberg, for Poland as well as for Germany.

TK: Without delving too deeply into the question of anniversaries – which art cannot tolerate – I would say just one thing: that cry was opportune.

KM: So Schmidt persuaded you to use his ideas, in this lightning-quick exchange?

TK: I persuaded myself, because my earliest inclinations had been to call up the image of that sinister object. And when Schmidt, sensing that he had struck fertile ground, started trying to talk me into the idea that Cricot and I should do something in Nüremberg and about Nüremberg because of the artistic links we had formed there, I answered that Stwosz's life and the fate of his art didn't particularly interest me. Especially since I have his finest work right under my nose, in Kraków, and I have no need to travel in order to convince myself of his stature.

KM: You were on the defensive against facile associations of ideas . . .

TK: And there was no shortage of them in Kraków and Nüremberg on the eve of Stwosz's anniversary. Some agreement or other was ratified, documents were signed, visits and return visits were arranged. And all at the expense of the poor artist everyone had suddenly remembered!

KM: Schmidt probably didn't think about all that anniversary business at all.

TK: Of course not. I was so put off by the artificial atmosphere of all that huffing and puffing that probably nothing would have happened, if it had not been for the turn that post-*vernissage* conversation had taken. Catherine joined in, and told me an anecdote which made me catch my breath.

KM: Did she lend support to your anti-anniversary sentiments?

TK: No. She just cited an instance from her gallery. While the building was being renovated, Catherine, as director, wanted to have some safety doors installed. In order to proceed with these changes, she had to get the agreement of the subtenants and neighbours. It so happens that the Galerie de France, established in one of the side streets close by, had long enjoyed the neighbourly presence of certain maiden ladies (gainfully employed). At a meeting called by Mme Thieck, one of these termagants, who remained unconvinced about the need to give special protection to any work of art, screamed: "Let the Artists Die!" All who were listening to Catherine's tale burst out laughing, and I said to Schmidt in delight: "I've got my title!"

KM: Your discovery has already become part of folklore. There's another story going round about a cleaning lady confronted by such chaos after a *vernissage* that she screamed these words in revenge.

TK: Mythologising this cry no longer has any mileage, because it is the discovery itself that should carry the day. On the other hand, things you discover in such circumstances are pretty fundamental.

I would like to outline the more general implications of my discovery of a title. As far as I'm concerned, the most significant factors in any work of art are instinct, the unconscious, and "automatism". I have noticed that whenever I begin to think about creating something new, a number of different elements come to hand. They fall into place without any direction or logic. And I don't know what to do with them. What is more, I always get the impression that these elements have been put in place by some unknown hand. I'm sure this hand is not the hand of God. I have no wish to interpret this in some metaphysical fashion; but I receive a lot of impulses, I pick up a lot of signals, and I feel that I have come so much closer to their ineffable source.

KM: And the question of the theory which accompanies the performance?

TK: It is early days yet for theorising. I'll have to come back to the question of the relation between theory and practice in my work; but in analysing the beginning of this process, I believe that within our consciousness, there are many "holes" waiting to be filled: new ideas, images and situations find their outlet via these "holes".

KM: If I understand you correctly, you are thinking of this period as a time when you store up energy, building a kind of "granary of images" or "warehouse of thoughts" . . . How do you behave during this "filling up" process?

TK: I have to psych myself up to endure as much as possible, and to maintain a completely open-minded attitude towards all the images I absorb and ideas I give room to. But the most important thing I have to believe is that those elements which at first seem ridiculously remote, in the end fit together and are connected in some way.

KM: It seems, then, that this grouping, merging, and even transubstantiating one image with another holds the key to the consciousness of the artist.

TK: Yes, in my case, the consciousness of randomness. "La Mossa del Cavallo" ("The Knight's Gambit"), as in chess, is the basis of the formation of metaphor. As in Futurist poetry.

The Common Room – an excellent novel by Zbigniew Uniłowski published in 1932 – nowadays says little to the average Polish reader.[2] Contemporaries, though, interpreted the intellectual-aesthetic implications of *The Common Room* in a variety of different ways. Bolesław Faron, the author of the only monographic study of the author, published in 1969, defines three representative critical attitudes.

> A large part of the most hot-headed critics . . . considered the novel to be the apotheosis of the thoughtless, unproductive lifestyle of a part of the literary generation of the thirties. Others maintain a quite opposite view, that *The Common Room* is a lampoon or pamphlet directed against the Bohemian lifestyle of the artists of the period. In the end, more moderate views emerged: Uniłowski's book was taken to be "a confession of a child of the time", and an exercise in self-knowledge and the definition of one's role in society.

The return to realism, which *The Common Room* bore witness to, was already being referred to as "the new objectivity". "This is the equivalent" – Stefan Kołaczkowski[3] observed – "to restoring to objective reality its dignity and worth".

"I have named this", he went on in his essay entitled *Polish Literature in 1932*, "a new accommodation to life, a new reconciliation with life, you might even call it a new sense of curiosity, the need to acknowledge life afresh from first principles, without prejudices or preconceptions."

"A calm readiness, a sober confrontation of the storm. This is the new 'realism'", affirmed Aniela Gruszecka,[4] in a critical debate with Kołaczkowski.

Kantor was fascinated by this *Neue Sachlichkeit*, this slow death of the artist under the eyes of his milieu, even with its unalloyed approval. Kantor's new thing was his Theatre of Death . . .

KM: You have spoken at length about Uniłowski's *Common Room* and the creative inspiration you found in it . . .

TK: The random function of chance played its part again and led me to Uniłowski's novel, where from the first scene to the last we witness the long, drawn-out death of the hero. Even more uncommonly, the author's own death is prefigured.

KM: In this new rehearsal you return to the realms of death and its workings. We have seen death already in *Dead Class* and *Wielopole, Wielopole*.

TK: The "domain" of death, which had attracted me for a long time, entered my theatre to very good effect. Not merely death, but its domain, a slow and implacable dying. A gradual, almost imperceptible process, unremitting, chronicled, transmitted to the spectators (because the theatre goes in for the tangibility of things) by a method of repetition to the point of sheer anguish. This is close to the world of "happening" art. Dying (death) in the theatre – starting with the Chinese and the Greeks – used to be a violent, dramatic, spectacularly finalising art. The punch line! A device that unfailingly guaranteed success, but was hopelessly threadbare. In this production I wanted dying to be the "binding" of various manifestations of life, almost constituting the *structure* of the whole.

KM: So Unilowski's text has an actual function on the stage?

TK: Unilowski's text is only a trace, an inspiration. The concept of a "scenario" loses its meaning in the course of my work, because it comes continuously into being . . . right to the end. I never know whether the sequence we are rehearsing will be the opening or concluding phase of the production.

The performance very often has to take shape during the course of the rehearsals, through the actors, their actions, their bodies, their feelings. We might be able to find in the performance from time to time distant echoes of this character or the remains of that literary text. But this is not because we are transferring a literary work to the stage. It has much more to do with my basic practice of not relying on some "constructed" or "composed" reality, but of operating with a "ready-made" (*prête*) reality, and with characters and objects which have been "found" (*objets trouvés*).

KM: Meaning?

TK: Lucjan, from *The Common Room*, is me . . . dying. But at the same time, in the hour of death, the domain of death demands that images of childhood make their appearance. My childhood . . . because the person lying on the death bed is me, and the little soldier in the kiddy-kart is me too, at the age of six. There is also my band of trusty followers, generals only (as in childhood dreams), who "look after" the child and with whom he plays.

Kantor's new scenic concept is a great treatise on dying. Is this the third and final part of the trilogy (after *Dead Class* and *Wielopole, Wielopole*), about the fate of the artist who – as one of Shakespeare's heroes says – "comes into the world in order to leave it"? Is it the "reckoning" the artist presents to the society he was born into, where he does his creative work, and where he dies? Or perhaps Kantor, selecting existential motifs which are already familiar from his art, ascribes to them now some completely unexpected meaning?

In any event the beginning – the place where the action is set – is a room with only one door . . .

KM: There is a room, but it is not – as it was in *Wielopole, Wielopole* – a space enclosed by a wooden layer of floor and the fragments of walls.

TK: The room has been continuously present in my imagination, and then in my art, since the wartime period of *The Return of Odysseus*. But it was not a question of merely implementing a spatial proposition, as was the case when the play had to be acted out in a real room, taken straight from the context of war, ruined and turned to rubble: it was something more than that.

KM: Were you thinking of the "snapshots of memory"?

TK: That certainly is a *sine qua non* for understanding my idea. This time there is no setting for the action as such, just snapshots of memory, developed one after the other. This "common room" becomes by turns a den of thieves; a shelter for an extraordinary band of artists and hoodlums; an emporium near a cemetery, whose inhabitants live there on the terms dictated by the objects hoarded; and a child's room, where a little lad amuses himself by exercising his imagination.

KM: The place has not been shaped, then according to the way the action of the plot develops?

TK: There is no plot in this production, nor can there be one. When we leave the "common room", the everyday inferno of our life, the spectacle grows of its own accord; its living material is the actor and everything that enters the orbit of his actions – thoughts, ideas, images, objects, and the place itself. This absence of a uniform plot, enclosed within calendar time in the form of the "circumstances" of the play, was what inclined me to devise the subtitle: "A Revue".

38. "The little soldier in the kiddy-kart is me at the age of six with a band of followers, made up – as in childhood dreams – of generals only." Kantor on the rehearsal of *Let the Artists Die!* Photo: Wojciech Kryński

One of the elements which inspired Kantor was the personage of Stwosz, the creative artist who had experienced well-earned fame in his lifetime. Sanctified upon the altar of public recognition and royally endowed by fortune, he knew the taste of artistic success. Yet shortly after his apotheosis in Kraków, he was subjected in Nüremberg to a succession of public insults and humiliations. Stigmatised for what were called fundamental errors, he spent the rest of his life struggling against the milieu in which he was fated to live and make his living.

KM: You said Stwosz interests you only for specific reasons which found an echo in your imagination.

TK: I take it you want to know how Stwosz came to get mixed up in this production of mine? It may surprise you, but I can tell you it came of its own accord. Stwosz is my *personage trouvé*. He makes his appearance in the middle of the performance to put to rights the chaos which has resulted from the collision of some of the "snapshots" from my room. Stwosz, moreover, takes the form of a *Młoda Polska*[5] sculptor, a decadent artist with one particular work of art in view.

39. One of the elements which inspired Kantor in his work on *Let the Artists Die!* was the personage of Wit Stwosz (Veit Stoss). Photo: Jacek Barcz

KM: What does it mean to say that Stwosz is a "found" character?

TK: I attach a deeper significance to the word "found". I am not implying any kind of discovery or search. A "found" object has links with fate, an "anterior" world, a "trans-sense" world, the domains of the dead I have talked about.

KM: Can you develop that a little?

TK: Yes. The theatre is, as far as I am concerned, a doorway through which the dead enter our lives.

KM: The consequence of their entrance is a transformation . . .

TK: Rather a sort of "impersonation". It's how I describe the actor's condition, as a state of death, in *Dead Class* and the Theatre of Death.

KM: The central episode is the building of the Altar.

TK: This building process, which makes indiscriminate use of the tenants of the "common room", is a contemporary Bohemia of dying and moribund artists, interspersed with the members of a theatre group who have forced their way illicitly into the room to act out their performance. This prepares the way for yet one more concept I wanted to demonstrate by means of this performance. This concept is the "prison", and it is bound up with the concept of the "work of art".

KM: You prepare the spectator for this sort of insight at the outset. Take the prologue, which might be called an "overture" by virtue of its musicality.

TK: The dead man, standing over an open grave, reminds us of a man on whom the prison doors have slammed shut. But if we return to the image of the Prologue: when the dead man exits, the living remain standing there for a long time . . . as if they can't accept the idea of leaving him alone "on the other side".

KM: Doubtlessly that is why they spend such a long time dressing him because it is his last "journey"; and why, kitted out and well padded, he starts out on the journey he will undertake alone. Then those who are responsible for his solitariness must be punished. Another newcomer from the beyond, this time a famous artist, takes his revenge on them by enclosing them in his work, which is a special form of atonement.

TK: By means of these events I wish to demonstrate my conviction that the work of art is a prison; and how utterly alien it is to the nature of Man.

KM: These wretched tenants, tortured by Stwosz, are subjected to exquisite sufferings in the pillory.

TK: In the sequence "The Work of Art as Prison", the actors are put in the pillory. In full view of the public. This isn't some proposition that I offer as a battle-cry, however. It is nothing less than the existential condition of the actor, his very existence, his state of being.

KM: What is more, the actors are bound up with objects from the outset: the Mother, with her small table and sunshade; the Identical Twins, with their bed, trolley, and chamber-pot; the Newcomer Artists; the Hanged Poet with his gallows/lavatory; the Artist Gambler with his own card-table; the Dishwasher with her sink; the Philology Student washing his dirty feet with water from a slop-basin.

TK: Taken as a whole, these objects recall a series of my drawings (or "con-
       ceptualisations") entitled "Man bound up with objects". Wrenched by
       force from these objects, they remain drawn out in convulsive attitudes,
       and with the chains binding them to the pillory they turn, for a while,
       into the living carvings of the St Mary's Church Altar in Kraków.

In the creative imagination of Cricot 2, yet another face appears as a source of
inspiration. This is the countenance of the founder and law-giver of the Polish
Legion, Józef Piłsudski, the symbol of Fame and Glory which every young
man dreams of. The figure of the Leader is seen through the eyes of a young
lad from secessionist Vienna who travels in his beloved kiddy-kart and plays
his savage games with the generals – who all take the form of tin soldiers –
and surround the Marshal. A specially intimate relationship with this image
is underlined by the "uncoupling" of the "ego" of the Master of Ceremonies
into four characters: the Artist who is present on stage, the six-year-old boy,

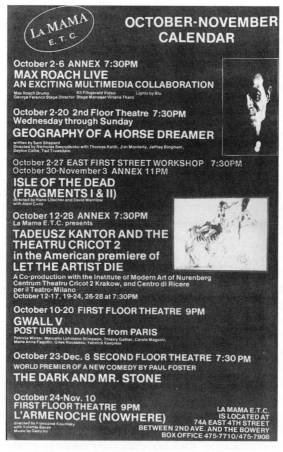

40. Advertising *Let the Artists Die!* at La Mama, New York, 1985. Photo: Jacek Barcz

and the two (dying) Identical Twins: the Hero (whose prototype is Lucjan in *The Common Room*) and the Author/Painter, who is modelled on Uniłowski. But the lad, dragging behind him the nightmare of the recollected image of Fame, instantly compromises it. The Leader rides the White Horse of the Apocalypse, whose glory and misery are symbolised by its white skeleton. Finally, the generals are automata which move with a mechanical motion, creeping like cockroaches around the common room.

TK: The Fame and Glory of the past are recognisable only in a fragmentary form. I grasped this when, fascinated by the Leader's funeral march, I became the owner of a damaged gramophone recording of this lofty and moving march, which made the piece both thrilling and repulsive at the same time.
       Grasping the idea of Glory unexpectedly became one of the topics of the performance. Who wins true fame? Only very few. As in life, so in art. Yet it is important for everyone to grasp the idea of Fame. To achieve it; to be fascinated by it; or quite simply to denounce it or scoff at it.

The artists crucified by Stwosz revolt: this revolt is acted out on the barricades, even in the Kantoresque Trenches of the Holy Trinity, from which the attack must be mounted . . . the attack on the public, which becomes a special way of settling accounts with the surrounding world and its art.

TK: What I have done, I have done for myself and my audience. Do I think this will be my last performance? At this moment, just before the first night, I'm absolutely certain of it.

Notes

1   Kantor seems to have conflated the Wagnerian story of the building of Valhalla (together with the sticky end of the giants who built it) and the (apocryphal?) story of the German-Polish artist Veit Stoss (Wit Stwosz) being stabbed in the cheek with a nail, in prison. A general fratricidal motif therefore hangs over this foray into Polish-German relations, quite appropriately.
2   Zbigniew Uniłowski (1909–1937), *Wspólny Pokój* (*The Common Room*). It must be said that there is a certain mystery about how or why Kantor came to make so much of this little-read book.
3   Stefan Kołaczkowski: professor of Polish Literature, one of the first commentators on Polish Modernism.
4   Aniela Gruszecka was a well-known Polish novelist writing before the Second World War.
5   *Młoda Polska* is a decadent/modernist tendency in Polish art, contemporary with the same trends in other countries, but marked additionally by a nationalist-revolutionary programme of a highly aestheticised type. *Młoda Polska* (*Young Poland*) stands alongside Modernism as a Polish art-form in the period from the end of positivism to the birth of independence in 1918, following the First World War. The name of the movement comes from the article *Młoda Polska* by Artur Górski, who was full of admiration for Stanisław Przybyszewski, the first Polish modernist and "gypsy" and who, in his declaration *Confiteor* (*I believe*), referred to the activities of groups of artists calling themselves "Young Germany" and "Young Scandinavia", in order to give voice to the necessity for revolution in art and tradition. *Młoda Polska* encompasses elements of modernism, symbolism, expressionism and impressionism in literature and in art.

14

I – THE MASTER

A documentary on the making of Kantor's
Let The Artists Die!
by Krzysztof Miklaszewski (1985–1986)

1. How should I represent Kantor working on a performance? Many methods have been tried already, but none so far has been equal to the task of representing the *milieu* of gossip around the preparations for each Cricot production. None has matched the atmosphere which, while enthralling and fascinating – was bound to exert a deeply disturbing power over the spectator. The title sequence, composed directly after the shooting, tries to establish the "five faces" of the Master, placed on record in the course of rehearsals. The first face: full of creative unrest, struggling with his material. "I entirely lose myself in all this", says Kantor. The second face: the despotic overseer. Some trouble on the technical side, in this case in the construction of the horse's skeleton, draws from Kantor a shower of objurgations directed at his loyal collaborators. The next face is Kantor the costumier, refining each set of outfits from the outset so that they might become a second skin to the actor. The director who tries to penetrate deeply into the physiology of the actor (in this case, the scene in which the Mother – Lila Krasicka – is seated in a chair); and the theoretician devising instant conclusions which arise from the process – these are probably the two most significant faces. This is precisely why we have to consider chance and luck as important factors in the creative process, and allow for a certain amount of irony in these "physiological" and "theoretical" processes.

2. The list of credits goes up, with a lively march phrase, a musical motif from *Let the Artists Die!*

3. The choice of literary material is crucial to Kantor, although – as he says himself – "writing a play for the theatre is just nonsense" (an aside directed at one of the sequences in his own production). Formerly, Kantor had always used Witkacy's texts, saying, "We don't play Witkacy, we play *with* Witkacy". From *Wielopole, Wielopole* onward, they become *actorly* texts arising from the theatrical situation, which have their origins in literature.

"They often ask me", said Kantor at his table in Kanonicza, "why I chose Uniłowski's *Common Room*; and I answer at once that I was simply interested in the room as such, and especially in the fact that it was *common*." The question of the location of the action is by no means a chance affair where Kantor is concerned. Light is thrown upon these questions, and especially their more complicated aspects ("This room is at once the room of my childhood, and the room of my death") by the new and crucial element of the persona of the creative artist. The Kantoresque "I" has been divided up here into four characters: one is the lad lying on the floor, dressed in a military cape – "Me at the age of six", says Kantor. This is brought into expressive focus by the camera shifting from the table to the floor, where sketches of the characters are lying. Then there is a shock of recognition when the panorama is extended, and the camera reveals the lad lying next to them. This figure is represented in minute detail from head to foot. When the camera is raised, we lift our eyes to the bed, where a man in black is lying. "That is me dying", says Kantor. The prototype of this character, however, is the poet Julian (Wacław Janicki) from Uniłowski's novel. Lying on the bed is his identical twin brother (Wacław's twin brother Lesław). Thus the author (Uniłowski) describes the death of his hero. Kantor tells us a little later that Uniłowski outlived his hero by scarcely two years. "Uniłowski actually described his own death, and that is what fascinated me most", said Kantor, taking up the challenge of demonstrating to spectators his Theory of Reflection. This is why he spends so much time with Leszek going over the changing expressions on the face of the dying man. Kantor, off-screen, giving an account of this dissociative process, remains engrossed in the situation of rehearsing the "portrait" of the dying man. Is Kantor showing the actor playing The Actor how he – like the painter – has to prepare his brother for the ceremony of dying? The fourth part of the Kantor "self" is Kantor in person, ever-present on the stage. This four-fold "split" of the ego is emphasised by the visit of the Actor/Doctor (Mirosława Rychlicka), who has been called to attend the sick man and has to make sense of this "splitting" to the audience. This leads to some amusing and theatrically engrossing moments. Kantor refers to the Doctor as a provincial quack (as in the story) and Aesculapius, the emissary of death (which he is in the performance). The Doctor becomes the butt of the comedy, and his "duel" with Kantor in the rehearsal is replete with Kantoresque black humour.

This unit, made up of 10 sequences, is an attempt to present the range of possibilities offered by the equation "I – Kantor".

4. Rehearsals with the actors are above all rehearsals of an *ensemble*. In this production, the collective scenes have a fundamental role in staging and interpretation. One element in the imagery is the effect of a closed "vicious circle" in which three groups come together: the tenants of the common room, gathered around the death bed; the Wandering Players who have irrupted into this den of thieves to act out a performance entitled *Let the Artists Die!*; and the General with his staff, seen through rose-tinted spectacles by the Young Lad who – as the preceding part of the film showed – is a characteristic projection of the dying man. One of these "integrative groupings" leads to the machinery being set in motion. The dramatic rehearsal, overseen by Kantor, points up the insufficiencies that remain from earlier phases of the production. When the group is first interrupted, it leads only to some points of interpretation. The second time Kantor orders the procession to come to a halt, he does so more forcefully, even grossly, insulting the actors and likening them to imbeciles. Kantor does have a proper reason as director for doing this, as the actors have still not finalised the scene they've been rehearsing. Another

41. A rehearsal of the running sequence with the Doctor (Mirosława Rychlicka) in *Let the Artists Die!* Photo: Wojciech Kryński

situation produces a similar set of stresses. This time it's a matter of the nervous intensity of facial mimicry Kantor demands on the part of the Owner of the Store by the Cemetery (Zbigniew Bednarczyk). The admonition directed at Bednarczyk, and via Bednarczyk at all the Cricot actors (who react very vividly to these assaults), is designed to shock. "You all have totally motionless necks! Can it be that the state of servitude you live in has caused your necks to atrophy?" Kantor demonstrates how his own neck is very mobile.

5. Trying on costumes, and the day-by-day alterations made to them, more or less constitutes the start of every rehearsal. For instance, we have to finish designing the costume of The Deceased (Bogdan Renczyński), a character whose somewhat picturesque dispatch is represented in its entirety at the beginning of the performance, in the so-called "Overture". Kantor starts by tearing the material to straighten the collar. When he is satisfied, he realises the outfit has no buttons. There follows a stream of invective on the subject of missing buttons, directed at the (absent) tailoress. The rehearsal, however, goes on. The Concierge–Cerberus (the author, Miklaszewski) hurries along The Deceased – as the "score" of the production demands – and the incident comes to a natural end. Definitively, since in this rehearsal the scene "takes" immediately – which gives Kantor a lot of satisfaction. Then we turn to the siren, which announces the march of The Deceased and the Concierge. This element, ultimately dropped from the production, seemed noteworthy to its proponents because of the Master's childlike reaction to it.

One of the succeeding rehearsals comes back to the problem of buttons. A rehearsal with the Storekeeper discloses the absence of buttons on yet another costume. This wrings an uncontrollable cry from the Master, who enjoins the tailoress to go and find herself . . . a tailor.

6. The irruption of the Wandering Players is connected with the arrival of the crates piled up by them on stage. This striking scene, which demands a lot of inventiveness and physical energy from the actors, is perfected at just that moment when all the effects are simultaneously synchronised. Moreover, all the participants use a specific verbal mannerism to introduce themselves and "transfix" the others. The Poet Decadent (Roman Siwulak), finding himself in the lavatory/gallows, sings street ballads. The Student of Philology (Jan Książek) washes his dirty feet, shouting at the top of his voice about what an achievement this is. The Concierge, who changes into a Publican (the author, Krzysztof Miklaszewski), pushes the Prostitute (Teresa Wełmińska) around on a crate, while she writhes in erotic ecstasy; and the Religious Bigot (Ewa Janicka) shouts endlessly "Mother of God! Mother of God!" All of this is played to the rhythm of a backstreet tango, with blaring, aggressive music. Kantor, sometimes unable to maintain control over the elements of a scene, liberally bestows insults upon his actors. Finally, the action dies away of its own accord, and The Deceased on the bed, who has also been caught up in these strenuous activities, announces the biographical "point" of this first part of the performance: "In this way, sixty-four years passed". Plus another six, in the shape of the Lad with the Military Collar (Leszek Stangret), who enters at this point to represent altogether the age of the Master – seventy.

7. With the sudden outburst of the hymn *Holy God, Almighty God*, the doors of the room open and Wit Stwosz (Andrzej Wełmiński) emerges – another projection of "I – Kantor". Kantor presents him as an artist whose task it is to create order, tidy things up.

8. The final phase of the Kraków rehearsals is characterised by Kantor's ever-growing pathological nervousness. The unfinished chair wheels cause an outburst of malice directed at the carpenter, while uncertainty about which actor enters when produces a real rumpus. Kantor, cursing the entire troupe, throws various objects – including glasses – at the carpenter, making him feel guilty with references to his poor state of health ("I could have a stroke! It would be the end of me."). He threatens to stop rehearsals, and turn down the personal invitation to Nüremberg, where the rehearsals are scheduled to continue. "I'm not going," says Kantor finally, in a fury. Packing up of scenery, costumes, props goes on constantly. When at last everything needed for the production has been stowed in crates, on one of them, written slowly with a large felt-tip pen, appears the comic inscription "Nürembug".

9. This inscription, together with the lovely Nüremberg poster advertising the world pre-première of *Let the Artists Die!*, tells us the group has adapted very well to its new surroundings, and that the rehearsals are moving towards their conclusion. The sense of making a clean break with the difficult Kraków period is emphasised by the music of a specially contrived military march (the second version of the musical *Leitmotiv* of the production).

10. The atmosphere of the dress rehearsal in Nüremberg's Kabel-Metal Werke Hall contrasts sharply with those that preceded it, by virtue of its almost idyllic mood. The dance of the Condemned Men with their Pillories, filmed

equidistantly from two camera positions, even draws praise from Kantor. But when the second scene unfolds, its fantastical scenarios taking place in a space formed by adapting the factory hall, the Master summons the rest of his strength and launches his first attack on the group. The moment the barricade is erected at the climax of the performance, the group is subjected to indiscriminate and vile abuse ("You really are just a bunch of dead donkeys!"), which is hard to tolerate. Kantor, in a physical frenzy, as if he was a mere stripling, no longer exerts complete control over the language of his performance, but in the most effective scene (which he has not yet completely worked out) he transgresses all the bounds of decency. When someone inadvertently piles an object on the shoulders of the most elderly of the actors while raising the barricade, it produces in him a murderous frenzy. This happens in respect of one of the Italian actors, who are playing the Generals. Their inept physical movements are a direct consequence of their nervousness at Kantor's provocations by drawing attention to his illness, and his vituperations, including some colourful folk expressions interspersed with outbursts in French ("All Italians are imbeciles"). His savage attack somewhat subdues the scenic effect he had been aiming for: the entry of the Condemned Men through the open doors, thrust onto the front of the stage, joined by the group as a whole jogging round the skeleton-horse, triumphantly led by the Marshal and the Young Lad. When they have completed their first tournée, the Prostitute sits on the horse, transformed into the Angel of Death and, at the head of the procession, moving them along, conducting and convulsing to the martial, dynamic rhythm of the march, is the Master himself.

11. The tranquillity seen clearly in the "image" of the other actors slowly approaching in other parts of the great hall, even the Young Lad (Michał Gorczyca), who is blowing soap bubbles, has come as a consequence of those pre-première stresses. Other actors who are still in the dressing-room are represented in different stages of make-up. The attention of Kantor's voice-over will be focused on that "image". Kantor has compared the actor to God the Creator and to . . . a hairdresser.

12. Kantor is already on stage, sitting in his chair and looking at the scaffolding of the auditorium towering massively above the hall, which is slowly filling with people. His gaze falls more and more nervously on the Tannoy, designed to implement his ideas about the spontaneous and intuitive character of the creative process At last, Kantor tears himself out of his chair and runs to the depths of the stage in the direction of the doors set back in the middle, giving the sign which will begin the performance. We then hear his dramatic confession, the *terminus ad quem* of this filmic representation: "I go in pursuit of myself. I create a secondary self. My work. This is a kind of frenzy." Kantor clicks his fingers in the air, claps his hands together and the spectacle – the product of many months of effort – begins. The doors open, the actors come out. My film is finished: the Master has had his way, his "I" has found its measure. In art.

13. The final credits come up, and in a mid-credit collage, recall the various faces of the Master.

15

A SIXTEEN-MINUTE
PRE-PREMIÈRE OVATION

On Sunday, 2 June 1985, in the old production hall of KME (Kabel-Metal-Elektro), spectators from Nüremberg and from all over the world had the opportunity to see something Kantor referred to simply as "A Revue".

Intended as a kind of settling of accounts with the outside world and a "life in art", this metaphysical "revue" involved images being set in motion, and superimposed. Kantor calls it "the slide show of memory". We are invited to enter through large doors the warehouse by the cemetery, then the den of thieves and the common room of the artistic fringe, and then a childhood room – and thus we experience the "seductive power of memory".

"In my view, memory is a particular structure which is like a 'lining' sewn into the present," said Kantor at a press conference; and he added: "The spectators who are going to watch this performance must not be persuaded into believing it is simply another journey into my own past. This past really has more to say about present times than my ruminations, which are shaped in the present moment".

A group of tenants of this "room that is not a room", dressed in black, dispatch the weird emanation of the dead man on his last journey. In this way, the prologue takes the form of serving a death sentence, which from now on will be implemented on stage by the laws of "the review". In the first scene, the Proprietor of the warehouse by the cemetery "calls up" all the tenants of the common room of artistic Bohemia. The sclerotic Mother, running *ad nauseam* through the lists of her relatives, and united by a schizoid bond with the man dying on the bed – "gives utterance" to the Author and the Hero, each a reflection of Kantor, who is already sitting on the stage.

When the machinery of this "everyday hell" is set in motion, the Young Lad turns up on his kiddy-kart. He is cast in the role of "little soldier boy", whom Kantor identifies as "Myself at the age of six." Traversing the entire acting space twice, the youngster endows it with the properties of a child's room and revives buried dreams which the adult soldier turns round in his mind. He recalls the more-or-less recognisable historical figure of Poland's great statesman and political idol, underlined by the melody emerging from "over there", which Poles will always associate with him. His name will never be mentioned because – as Kantor rightly says – "that would be over-literal, and would shift the interpretation of this conflict on to a historical plane".[1] And above all it is a plot about the Young Lad's dreams of military glory.

42. Tadeusz Kantor. Photo: Wojciech Kryński

That is why, after a short while, the childish imagination dictates that the grown-up soldier should get on a horse, while his attendants take on the role of generals, climbing out of every corner of the room, kitted out like tin soldiers. The Young Lad, in keeping with the spirit of the game, "manipulates" this weird soldier.

When Kantor takes these "slides" of his life and adds the ever-present image of the cemetery-warehouse, then the dying man's room and the childhood room are transformed into a proper den of thieves. It is the group of actors who bring this about, eager to act out *Let the Artists Die!* in the common room. In the Actors, alongside the Concièrge (from the prologue), are the bizarre Barman and the Bored Individual who sings old tangos in his lavatory/gallows, the Student obsessed with washing his feet, and the Card Sharp who is stuck in his own card-table. The real star of the group is an attractive Prostitute, plying for trade and making the Religious Bigot, with her huge rosary, feel even more frustrated.

The entrance of this group of shady artistes signifies their penetration into the space of the common room, which comes to represent an inferno of everyday squalor. The intrusive frames bring about the transformation of the Warehouseman into a filthy Washerwoman; and the weird Barman assumes the attire of degraded Artist, calling to mind Wit Stwosz, the inspiration for the Nüremberg/Kraków *genius loci*. Stwosz is eager to compose his great work of art all over again, remembering, as if "from life", the altar of St Mary's in Kraków.

This work will reach the eyes of the spectators in a special way. The thugs brought in by the Artist and Concièrge will chain the tenants to a refined torture machine or pillory, and by means of this torment will arrive at the expressive poses seen in the carvings of the altar. This is not the end: the conflict of the artists and the prisoners will lead them to the barricades. The Kantoresque Entrenchments of the Holy Trinity are the meeting place for all those who dwell in the creative imagination: and from there they will attack . . . the spectators, who are propelled by the imperative contained in the title, *Let the Artists Die!*

This is just one interpretation of Kantor's profoundly ambiguous performance, which unfolds at an incredible tempo, passing through a series of changes in the imaginative-metaphoric process that occurs during immediate contact with the viewer. In the course of the one hour, thirteen minute pre-première, no-one in the audience so much as stirred in their seat. It is not surprising that the applause of the public, stunned by the show as a whole, lasted sixteen minutes.

Notes

1   Although Kantor cleverly masked it, the inspiration for this piece is clearly Marshal Józef Piłsudski, the acclaimed leader who brought about the rebirth of Poland following the First World War and was officially branded an Enemy of Communism by the Government of People's Poland, 1946–1989.

16

DID I HELP OR DID I HINDER?

(Conversation, July 1986)

The famous Renato Palazzi, the uncompromising Milanese critic who for a short while was chancellor of the Civica Scuola D'Arte Drammatica, used to give his graduating students – budding actors, directors and scenographers – an additional test. This was to work alongside Kantor: thus giving his students the chance to exercise their creative powers under the tutelage of an artist Palazzi admired enormously. Kantor, for his part, agreed to take on all the pedagogical chores, and to give a series of lectures backed up by practical exercises. That's how the Milan "diploma" performance was born: introduced with the support of an outstanding Polish artist. His title – *A Marriage* – is also connected with Kantor's vision of the Cricotage *Où Sont les Neiges d'Antan?*, as indeed are those sequences of *Wielopole, Wielopole* which had their origin in Italy (work on this production took place in Florence). *A Marriage* has the subtitle "In the Constructivist and Surrealist Manner".

KM: Your biography informs us that you embarked on a career as a teacher more then once. You were twice thrown out of the Kraków Academy of Fine Art, and turned down the proposal of permanent work from the PWST[1] in Kraków to teach future directors after a trial period of two years. This sets the scene for your appointment as Visiting Professor of Painting in Hamburg. These are just the bare facts. What lies behind them, speaking as someone who has worked with you for umpteen years, is your true significance as a teacher. There never was a time when you failed to take advantage of your encounters with students or conversations with young people regardless of time or place.

TK: You are obviously right to imply that teachers are born, not made. My position is as follows: my art has more to it than meets the eye. This is its doctrine, its message, which is aimed at the "receiver". The spectators I value most are the young spectators, just embarking on life. Their active involvement will help determine not just the shape of their lives and beyond, it will also determine the role art will play for them. All artists – and I am thinking, of course, of good artists, those who matter – must be teachers, even if their public statements – which they once held against me in Poland – are hard to understand or even anti-pedagogical.

KM: There is also the second duty of artists to interpret their own art, and evaluate its context.

TK: Conscious awareness of one's own activities, as well as the analysis of the works of others – indispensable to the understanding of a historical moment – are also basic teacherly traits. The fact that I am always referring back to the context in which I live and work is by no means a matter of chance. It is also worth mentioning that my perspective on things has made me many enemies in the artistic context. Artists are in the habit of talking only about themselves, and then imagine, naively, that everything the world dishes up is something they invented. Tradition is a category which has the power to check and correct such a narrow perspective. I would go so far as to say that the propagation of a perspective like this among art's receivers is a fundamental obligation of the artist, who on account of his *métier* is at the same time a teacher.

KM: Don't the ideas of "artist-as-pedagogue", and "pedagogue" as in "school", cancel each other out?

TK: Partly. In my pronouncements, I have tried to emphasise my distrust of all schools of art.

KM: Your own as well?

TK: That too. But what I am talking about now is more the idea of school as an institution, a school which has the ambition of teaching art. However, art can't be taught . . .

KM: But it *can* educate people and prepare them for work, even for artistic work.

TK: Yes, I agree. Academies of Fine Art bear witness to this, at least, academies as they once were. But as I recall, in places of learning not bearing the inscription "higher", the relationship between master and pupil, or teacher and taught, is like the relationship between apprentice and craftsman. Great teachers used to have great students. Nowadays, alas, it is quite different.

KM: And theatre school?

TK: Here, I'm afraid, things are even worse. Theatre schools by and large have tunnel vision, they don't communicate an understanding of art as a whole. Every balanced observer knows that the art of the actor is not separate from art as a whole, and it cannot be separated. The art revolutions of the early 20th century emphasised these strict sets of interdependencies.

KM: We live in an age of increasing specialisation.

TK: In art such an idea is deadly.

KM: Didn't you decide to work in a specialised theatre school?

TK: After the Kraków school, I had another try. Because the first had worked out so badly, I set great store by the second.

KM: Why Italy?

TK: Apart from the exceptional interest in my art in that country, the deciding factor was my experience of working on *Wielopole, Wielopole* in Florence. As well as having rehearsals there with my Polish group in 1980, I gave lectures and demonstrations for Italian students. From the students on that course grew the Italian part of Cricot 2. An added endorsement was given by Palazzi, a splendid critic, who understands my work absolutely.

KM: What was the first meeting with your students like?

TK: Terrible. It confirmed my worst fears . . . My optimism drained away rapidly as I watched the short sketch I had asked them to prepare. The theme was free choice, as was the form. Everything therefore depended on their inventiveness, taste, and understanding of the stage. I almost had a fit; in a scene lasting a few minutes, I was confronted with everything I had been battling against for years in the theatre: imitation and mimicry, falsity and bad taste, the predominance of "the word" over other theatrical components, pretentiousness and artifice. I was horror-struck and – of course – enraged. But when I began to talk to them and draw them out, I became convinced that it was only partly their fault. That is how they were trained, that is what had been asked of them. When I got over my initial anger, I told them quietly they had to start again . . . from the beginning.

KM: I'm sure this shocked them, since they had already graduated!

TK: It did shock them a little, but it was really the first time they had heard words like these, and they listened: they listened with fascination. What's more, this fascination kept growing. After a while, thanks to their receptiveness and dedication, I realised I could begin to work with them in earnest.

KM: This must be why you named your twenty-two examples and accompanying exercises an "Elementary Theatre School".

TK: Yes. I told them they must begin their education again from the beginning – from elementary school. And as far as I'm concerned, "elementary school" means a knowledge of the traditions of art.

KM: Which moments in that tradition did you revisit?

TK: I went back to Constructivism and Surrealim, the movements in twentieth-century art which I value most, and which I feel brought about the most radical changes. It goes without saying that it wasn't my intention, in 1986, to simply repeat them. But reconstructing and developing ideas can be unbelievably educational as well as – more importantly – inspiring . . .

KM: Your "Elementary Theatre School" embodies the very idea you had discarded, the idea of "school".

TK: Yes, I capitulated, and chucked the word "school" at them. "You have to study." I screamed at them, "because you know nothing, and what you *have* learned is just getting in your way, it is hampering you on your journey towards art."

KM: So that's how it started.

TK: But then the problems began . . .

KM: What sort of problems?

TK: The problems I had understanding *them*. I knew if I couldn't understand their mentality, and couldn't illuminate their imaginations, teaching was meaningless. I just couldn't get through to them.

KM: So what did you do about it?

TK: I gave a course of lectures, but during the practical exercises, I tried to give them a wide margin. I waited for them to open up. And it soon turned out that they were catching on amazingly fast. That truncated course was over before you could say "Jack Robinson". And on top of it was the work they had to produce.

KM: Did you work differently from the way you had worked in Cricot?

TK: I used the methods of teaching in an artist's studio. I would throw out some subject and draw up some blueprint. The rest was their business. The subject was the situation of a marriage ceremony; the blueprints were supplied by the actors, who took on the roles and identities of members of the two families (the bride's and the groom's). My business was – as in the workshop – to correct what they had done.

KM: I am still under the spell of that video, which you brought with you, containing a recording of the "diploma production" – though unfortunately a very amateurish one. It consists of two sketches, each given a completely different form. The first is "constructivist", the other is "surrealist". This was the orientation which decided how the actor performed, his gestures, the range of expressions – and this you "threw" at your students.

TK: I had to be consistent. I wanted the performance to embody all the research and exercises I had laid on my audience. Hence the significant experiment of placing them in two situations, which led in the directions indicated. The exercises in Constructivism, based more or less on the designs of the Russian scenographer Liubov Popova,[2] were followed by a surrealist narrative version which revealed what happened next, after the death of the married couple.

I tried to infect my students with a faith in avant-garde art, the art which Cricot exemplified. Whether I have succeeded or not we shall see in a few years' time. For the time being, all my students have found work in "normal" theatres which – as we know – take these matters very lightly. But – as the Scriptures say – a drop can turn the balance.

KM: There were standing ovations at the performances. As if it was not enough that all your students got jobs in the theatre, which is very difficult in Italy, they also won prizes at a student festival. It's pretty clear how successful your efforts as a teacher were.

TK: So much the worse, because I do not know to this day whether I was more of a help or a hindrance to those impressionable young people, whom I marvel at, from a perspective of just a few weeks.

Notes

1 PWST – the State University School of Dramatic Art.
2 Liubov Popova (1889–1924) died during a post-revolutionary epidemic. A major designer and painter, whose work was drawn upon by Meyerhold and admired (and to some degree imitated) by Tatlin, Popova's phenomenal sense of space and colour have only quite recently been properly recognised.

17

EXEGI MONUMENTUM, OR *THE MACHINE OF LOVE AND DEATH*

(Description in dialogue form, July 1987)

On 13 June in Kassel, during the theatre festival which ran in tandem with the contemporary art exhibition *Documenta 8*, Kantor mounted the world pre-première of his "Cricotage with dolls, carvings, objects, and machinery", *The Machine of Love and Death*. After two performances in five days, the Cricotage was repeated in Milan . . . and played ten times.

KM: The *Machine of Love and Death* originates from Maurice Maeterlinck's *The Death of Tintagiles*.[1]

TK: Yes. Maeterlinck's original plot is concerned with Igraine and Bellegère, two sisters living on an island ruled by a treacherous Queen, who, after devouring all the men of her household, forms the intention of eliminating the sisters' younger brother, Tintagiles. With the help of their faithful old servant Agolval, Igraine and Bellegère engage in a deadly battle with the brutal Queen's servants. But the play ends with the victory of the Queen, and the death of the sisters.

The single visual representation consists of the extending metal doors, set in motion by a melody which is accentuated by the presence of the pitiless Tyrant. The doors part and display the mechanical gadgetry of three obedient *Übermarionetten*, performing their movements in a mechanical fashion in time to the melody. The dramatic business begins with four actors coming on in dark clothes. These are the Attendants, who bring in chairs and place on them the wooden marionettes, which represent the two sisters and their little brother, Tintagiles. The Attendants are given orders through a loudspeaker, but they don't altogether understand the text, which is essentially poetic. Before embarking on any action, they try to translate it into a language of everyday gestures. This produces a semantic hiatus, intensifying the sense of stress. Meanwhile, the seating and shifting of the marionettes with wooden sticks produces an effect of geometrified *gestus*, à la Bauhaus.

KM: You staged a production of Maeterlinck's play as much as half a century ago.

TK: Exactly fifty years ago I produced *The Death of Tintagiles* in the manner of a puppet show. At that time I was completely besotted by abstractionism, I worshipped Malevich, Mondrian, Klee, I was full of enthusiasm for the pure forms created by Gropius, Moholy-Nagy and Schlemmer . . .

KM: You were a constructivist . . .

TK: Yes. I was a constructivist, but even then I was already troubled by doubt as to where the great mysteries of Maeterlinck's plays fitted in. Even then I wondered what I was looking for in the crypts of Polish kings, or backyards full of rubbish and nettles where the poetry of Schulz lives on . . .

KM: How many times was the pre-war production of *The Death of Tintagiles* put on?

TK: Only once. I am going back to it now and making the first part of my Cricotage out of it. *The Machine of Love and Death* consists of two parts. It is intended to link up my past with my present, and it is conceived as a sort of confrontation between myself and history.

The Queen's Secret Policeman monitors the behaviour of the Attendants. This gloomy individual is played by Stanisław Rychlicki, the only Pole in the six-strong Italian team, among whom it is easy to make out Kantor's protégés from Florence who performed in *Wielopole, Wielopole* and *Let the Artists Die!* Thanks to the vigilance of the Secret Policeman, the inexorable mechanical Maids keep rhythmically reappearing like a sort of portent; then the Queen is led on stage, where – like a disagreeable traveller – she packs the marionette of little Tintagiles into her suitcase. When she's gone, the Secret Policeman clears up the space, and when the doors open for the last time, Kantor's voice utters an authorial pronouncement from the loudspeaker: "No more Sacred Abstraction".

KM: The first part of your Cricotage reproduces that performance in every detail. It is not only the ideas that are important, but the materials too: wood and metal. What about the second part?

TK: If we go back to the performance I devised while still a student at the Kraków Fine Art Academy, and add the present moment (1987) as a second part – this is a time when abstraction, which once broke all bonds with symbolism, has to surrender its pride of place . . .

KM: Are you thinking of the symbolism of the author of *The Death of Tintagiles*?

TK: Maeterlinck is grounded in reality . . .

The change in the music of the second part is integrally linked with the transformation of the representational process. The shepherd, brought to life from a painting by Wojtkiewicz, and the fair-haired girl in white, become the Hero and Heroine of the nuptials. This is death's matchmaking, accompanied by a wooden horse; in the sound dimension, a wedding song begins to dominate the proceedings, imported from the folklore of southern Italy. The lad, who is going wild on his horse, tirelessly parades past his bride, who is dragged along by witches of the kind depicted by Goya. The words of the wedding song, *O Mother, Take Me to My Betrothed*, underline the counterpoint of the situation: the clash of two processions.

KM: Is it possible to make a real love machine?

TK: No.

KM: And a death machine?

TK: Maybe. The machine is no longer a machine, though. It's just something that does its job.

During the first half of the performance Kantor is sitting at one side of the stage. He is dressed in black as usual, like a director and creative artist wholly caught up in the "journey" of his art. In the second part he becomes an actor. When the box covered in black cloth is raised, women's feet and arms stick out of it. But when a real woman of flesh and blood appears, Kantor, attentive and correct, wraps her in a shroud. After this "solo" performance, the actors join him and begin their march in a circle around the metal door. After a while, Kantor gestures to them to stop. They stop: gravediggers and viragos, marionettes and all the rest. However, they only stop for a while. Soon the march moves on, to make progress ad infinitum. The way Eros and Thanatos promenade through our lives.

> This spectacle is hard to describe, but something *does* happen – it radiates a fascinating, ever-changing power. We can learn from Kantor the meaning of the words magic, enchantment, bewitchment. What is going on here is acted out in a reality in between love and death.
>
> Lothar Orzechowski, *Hessische Allgemeine*, 15 June 1987.

> The procession stamps the seal of its splendid image on the whole production. The Kantoresque imagination moves with the tempo of a funeral march, in which a weird projection of childhood is combined with the idea of inexorable control.
>
> Francesca Bonanni, *Il Timpo*, 21 June 1987.

> In the course of less than an hour of tempestuous, shifting images, amidst processions of phantoms and the living-dead, on a stage dominated by organised chaos, Kantor as demiurge, acting out once again the part of a dumb conductor, gesticulating charismatically over his mob of heroes, examines and sifts feelings and moral anxieties. It seems, however, that on this occasion, from the profoundest pessimism of his metaphor there comes a ray, if not of hope, then at least of charity and compassion. This is much more a machine of love than a machine of death.
>
> Domenico Rigotti, *Avvenire*, 20 June 1987.

TK: How does the poet put it? "Exegi monumentum . . ." What is the most important thing for me, in the sum total of my activities, at the moment when I have admitted to myself that I am growing old? To leave behind a trace, a memory, something that is not immediately forgotten and blotted out by this world, which so quickly disposes of everything . . .

Notes

1 The Belgian Nobel Prize-winning playwright Maurice Maeterlinck (1862–1949) inspired the Russian director Meyerhold to find "biomechanical" equivalents for his strange, abstract configurations of spatial and personal relations. His *Pelléas et Mélisande* provided the text for Debussy's great opera, which is peculiarly true to the "anti-psychological" symbolist tendencies of the original.

18

"... NOTHING FURTHER ..."

(Notes from conversations, March 1988)

KM: Your last exhibition, which you put on for friends and acquaintances in the wretched little "Cricoteca" cellar, was attended by the whole of Kraków, and some trusty Warsaw-ites as well, led by Artur Sandauer. It is entitled "Nothing Further".[1]

TK: When I spend time sorting out my notes on all the different roads I have travelled in my artistic life, there are moments I look at in precisely that spirit . . . and since I have resolved to conceal nothing, I admit that in moments like these I lost faith in the existence of any continuation . . . Nothing Further. This phrase will be repeated many times in my life. Moments of doubt, for sure, but as soon as I give utterance to this nihilistic phrase, I always feel fine. Despair gives me tremendous strength: never to surrender!

KM: Do those doubts, which seem to crystallize into an unshakeable resolve to pursue your journey into the unknown, also provide you with the power to make significant changes in the development of your art?

TK: Yes, and what is even stranger, those doubts tend to be disguised each time by my innovations. At some stage, life irrupted into the sad little Backroom of my Imagination and took control there, as if exacting vengeance for my impertinence in making use of its refuse and miserable leftovers, rather than its fine fullness of being. There was a mass of setbacks and disasters ready and waiting for the next stage of my life. In despair, I hid in all the corners of my poor little room . . . "Nothing further", I cried, I cursed the very image I had believed in for so long. I made a crazy decision to get out of all this, once and for all. I was not taking flight: it was a premeditated dereliction of a place of privilege, an admission of disastrous failure. The role of clown really attracted me. That's the way it always is in my theatre. Inside the Showman's Booth.

The performance has ended, everyone has left, and by the entrance stands old Pierrot, his face stained with tears, waiting for his Columbine, who has long since gone off to her favourite hotel . . . "Nothing Further . . ."

An appropriate ending for this Theatre of Life, whose epilogue is my last picture: "Here I Come to Rest".

KM: Those phrases you keep using are the titles of pictures in your extraordinary exhibition. In the first, which you are discussing, someone –

43. Tadeusz Kantor. Photo: Jacek Barcz

that is, yourself, as the picture's originator – is emerging from the picture. The second underlines the motif of remaining somewhere forever, or in other words . . .

TK: Death. But the painting has to end up victorious! What's more, this isn't a *vernissage*; those eight pictures, which communicate my way of thinking . . .

KM: And the state of your soul . . .

TK: Yes . . . and the state of my soul . . . they are only trying to show – those who want to know – what I am actually doing, and what I have done.

KM: *I'll Come Again No More*. That's the title of the performance you are working on at the moment. The title is at once shocking and eloquent, like the title of the exhibition. Would you be willing to lift the veil from the secret?

TK: None too willingly, but here goes: the action is set in a squalid pub, a low dive where the spectres of my theatre, from the period of *Balladyna* and *The Return of Odysseus*, have gathered. A conversation like this ought to have a point, but I don't want to disclose it yet. The whole production is ready, but I don't know how many things will be changed. You will recall this from working on *Let the Artists Die!* I am very conscious how many splendid scenes I dropped from it. I have tried to forget about it altogether. I'm terrified that as soon as I start work on the crucial rehearsals in Milan, the same thing will happen.

KM: Does this mean you foresee radical changes to what was seen by spectators in the rehearsals?

TK: The basic components will doubtless remain, and the general circumstances. Otherwise the work we have done so far would become meaningless. You were right to ask, immediately before the opening of the exhibition, about the new performance. That work is interwoven with my thoughts about the theatre. It's as though I wasn't painting, but putting on a play. I have been painting as if I wasn't thinking about painting. Yet it seems to me that everything is interwoven. All part of the same process of thinking.

KM: I hear that you have been writing a theoretical piece which is very important to you.

TK: A new synthesis... designed for the Centre Pompidou catalogue, and bound up with my preparations for this production. It is called *My Encounters with Death*. Here I must add that a lot has been written, and is still being written, about my obsession with death. The things people attribute to me in connection with this, I really can't make head or tail of... but the fact of the matter, as far as I'm concerned, is the concept of death itself, and the existence of this concept in all my work.

KM: Meaning...?

TK: The symbolism of death is central to almost all my ideas. This concept applies equally to my artistic output. Thinking about my past, I once wrote:

> The time of theatre is at hand. Suddenly she appeared (i.e., Death), flitting through the wings and leaving on the stage her theatrical coffin. An artist settles down on it with his two dead wives.

44. Tadeusz Kantor. Photo: Jacek Barcz

TK: I speak of Witkacy's *Cuttlefish* – the Dictator and the Pope. And the artistic session has begun its work. But the dominant figure is She who Cannot be Seen.

> From that time on, she appeared regularly on the stage, a tragic figure who has elevated her miserable relics to the level of real pathos. Sneering, she has swept away with a laugh everything that is small and ordinary. Little by little, she has become my friend. She has been standing behind the scenes, in stony silence, with her beautiful face . . .

TK: . . . and so on and so forth . . .
      I watched, fascinated, how she did everything: Life in the frenzied, tempestuous and magnificent dissolution of its everyday round disclosed at bottom its hidden truth. And that was Her truth. Unbearable. And what then? Just listen to this:

> The Groom was contracted in marriage to the dead Bride. Thrown unpityingly into a corner, dragged into the wedding ceremony by the Priest, she promised to love, honour, and obey for good or for ill. And then, when the pitiful wedding ceremony was over, the betrothed took the dead body in his arms and tugged it over the ground, back into life.

KM: That's *Wielopole, Wielopole* . . .
TK: But in another context:

> She did not spare anyone, even herself. She changed into the wretched Cleaning Woman employed by a miserable schoolroom, with a kitchen broom in the place of her medieval scythe. That's how sure she was of her apotheosis.

KM: That's *Dead Class*.
TK: And my final quotation:

> When the Great Marshal paraded on his beloved horse – now nothing but bones – to the acclaim of his generals, who rose at his bidding from tombs and from cemeteries, I saw Her, too, on another horse, in a grey universal triumph. And the moment came when, choking on her triumph, she ventured on the ultimate blasphemy. That's when I saw Her behind the scenes. There was nothing of that triumph about her then. She had become simpler and more intense, as if demonstrating a truth that was hard to bear and that went very deep. On-stage, her handiwork bore fruit in prison. In the Condemned Cell.

KM: You took a decision to appear alongside your actors in this new production. Not in person this time, but from the sidelines, from the position both of creator and the most critical of spectators . . .
TK: Yes. I am generating a text which – as I see it – will define the axle on which the whole thing rotates.

KM: Will you be an actor then?

TK: No. I will be myself. But I will be with the actors.

KM: At a certain moment, the characters who appear in the dive are surrounded by Nazi officers.

TK: This is directly linked to *The Return of Odysseus* – the whole play will be a sort of resumé of my pilgrimage. But then, during the occupation, we did not take on board the fact that like the actors, we really were "surrounded" by the Nazis.

KM: Is this just a historical retrospective of a visual motif generated from circumambient reality?

TK: Yes. But there's something more. The Nazi group introduced into the performance is defamiliarised. The weapons they carry are not rifles and pistols, but violins.

KM: Uncle Stasio, the deportee from *Wielopole, Wielopole*, came back from the war with a dilapidated violin case which he dragged like a broken wing, and from this case, by turning a handle, he extracted the strains of a Chopin Scherzo.[2]

TK: Here it functions in the opposite way.

KM: We know, of course, that in one of the death camps an orchestra played while an execution was in progress.

TK: My imagination was working along those lines . . . Nazi officers, in the smartest of smart outfits, appear with violins in their hands to the rhythm of a tango. They appear, moreover, at the Last Judgement, which is slowly taking shape in the dive . . .

KM: Though its starting-point . . .

TK: Is a get-together to mark an anniversary.

TK: Everything I have created up to now has had a confessional dimension. The confessions have become more and more personal, to save things from oblivion. Confessions born out of nostalgia, out of a longing to return to childhood, to preserve the happy days of childhood. Later, to save my childhood room, my family room. To make it endure as part of the great spiritual history of our culture. And then that insatiable desire or fantasy or cry for art to be free, to be governed only by me, my weaknesses, my frenzies, my sicknesses, my calamities, my solitude . . .

TK: What to do after directing *Let the Artists Die!* At first I did not know, as usual.

KM: And into the gap in your thinking slipped the thought ". . . Nothing Further . . ."

TK: I began from a gradual return to the past, where all those different characters, different events and different actions appear. I went back as far as the war, to my *Balladyna* and *The Return of Odysseus*. And indeed, if these had not been my private experiences, I would have stopped working altogether, because to return to the past without the luggage of contemporaneity would not have held much interest on its own account.

KM: There you touch upon a particularly sensitive point, which is the problem, where our psychological makeup is concerned, of transposing our personal experiences into the domain of art.

TK: Yes, really, a philistine, bourgeois mentality ... A pious mentality ... any mentality that is exceptionally deep-seated. All of this just comes across as inflexibility, if not as miserable exhibitionism ... In contradistinction to all this, I think that in the process of transposing your most intimate experiences into art, you have a moment of shame, but this is already a very good thing. In other words, you can set out along this road, and some artistic effect is bound to follow. But if your creative doubts begin to ascend to the level of feeling ashamed of yourself, that's when your work starts getting interesting.

KM: Once upon a time – in the religious context – public confessions of sin were a form of purification. In the artistic context, it's mainly the artist who is involved. The theatre, however, was formed in the public domain.

TK: In the public highway – *vis-à-vis* the common herd – the worst things are dragged into the light of day, as well as the most sacred. So in my next re-run ...

KM: *Vis-à-vis* the imperative "Nothing Further ..."

TK: That's really what interested me. My private being. But that "private" self isn't enough on its own. It calls for vindication. In art, it has to be vindicated by artistic means.

KM: I'm sure you recall how a public confession can also serve to stir up trouble. Doubtless this has inspired you for those who have ears to hear.

TK: As the famous Italian critic Renato Palazzi wrote about me. "This is yet one more rupture in the lovely skin of our civilisation." But, that apart – what more is there to say? I've come to the end of my theatrical games ... and in this annexation of my fantastical intimacies, I see my dramatic trump card.

KM: Let's go back to the situation in your performance (*I'll Come Again No More*) when those characters – the Cricot *dramatis personae* – come into the dive ...

TK: It is a dive of the worst type ... a dive with a despotic manager-cum-restaurateur ... a dive with a Jewish skivvy who is always washing the floor when she's not granting sexual favours to the customers. A gang of derelicts calls in ... the only elegantly-dressed customer is me. I'm having a black outfit made. I'm wearing a hat, a scarf, a spotless white shirt. I opt for this attire in an effort to ... denigrate myself. It is not a way of setting myself above the others, but of turning myself into a sort of poseur.

KM: Without dwelling on the details, which – as you have quite rightly emphasised – may still change many times, what is the essence of this production?

TK: The essence is to strip away all the outer layers, the polished, elegant layers which are equated with the high moral standing of an individual, and lay bare to the public gaze all the true features of private identity.

KM: We're still talking about two scenes in the production. The first is where the gang comes in. Is it designed to be the same as the one which haunts the "common room" in *Let the Artists Die!*?

TK: Yes, this is the same gang of pimps, prostitutes, and human debris under the banner – as I pointed out many years ago – of François Villon, performing in my new production a remembered version of *The Return of Odysseus*. I had returned in my mind to that wartime production. *The Return of Odysseus* will be acted out like a bit of tomfoolery with a Greek lesson and some school benches . . .

KM: Are those the benches from *Dead Class*?

TK: Absolutely. They will perform on those benches, which have been borrowed from the other "session", and they will be seated in them in the same fashion. And then comes the second of my entrées: the arrival of the Nazis. At first, they will be sitting in the audience. They may even applaud a little. But just one look from them is enough, they don't have to shoot.

KM: Which of those characters on the benches is from your past?

TK: The Rabbi, of course, who will conduct the Nazi orchestra, the filthy, begrimed Rabbi from *Wielopole, Wielopole*, the cornerboy from *The Water Hen*, the Identical Jewish Twins with their "Board of Ultimate Salvation", also from *The Water Hen*. Another named character from that era of events and happenings will also make an appearance.

TK: When someone is really very unhappy, they summon up colossal inner forces. You almost have to cultivate this inward state of wretchedness. First unhappiness, and then – that inner strength.

TK: My role at the moment, in my capacity as "man of the theatre", consists of objectifying everything I experience in my private life. So that it all stays personal. At the same time I realise that the misfortunes of a stranger are of absolutely no concern. People will just laugh, or tap their foreheads knowingly. So I have to "construct" this element in such a way as to make it interesting to others, and hence to me . . . as an artist.

KM: We have been talking about conjuring up a succession of characters from the Cricot past. You also spoke about the duplication of situations. The Greek tomfoolery is of course a repetition of the stuff (the old men back at school) we find in *Dead Class*.

TK: There will also be a wedding service, conducted by a clergyman from a medieval cathedral. It will take place in the dive, of course. But when he goes into the dive, a tango tune is playing non-stop. The tango is a sort of trap for the newcomer. He begins to dance, back and forth. The restaurateur tries in vain to call him to order because the happy couple are due to make their appearance. In desperation, he has to dispense the sacrament himself, unable to restrain the mad priest.

KM: What do the young couple look like?

TK: On a remote-control trolley are the dummy, which represents me, and the coffin. The restaurateur ineptly repeats a set phrase from *Wielopole, Wielopole*, while the capering priest keeps correcting the ceremony.

KM: *The Water Hen, Dead Class, Wielopole, Wielopole, Let the Artists Die!*, and even *The Return of Odysseus* are the raw materials of your visual and dramatic inspiration.

TK: The entire oeuvre, you might say . . . a couple of cardinals also put in an appearance from the Cricotage *Where are the Snows of Yesteryear?* These cardinals will have the air of having seen better days. The faded red of their costumes clearly indicates how worn they have become. What's more, the cardinals, who once danced so beautifully and with such precision, will keep falling over and dropping helplessly to the ground, out of step and out of time. I will be secretive and say nothing about the outcome of the procession, crowned by the ceremony of the aborted wedding.

KM: And what about you: what are you doing all this time?

TK: I sit on the stage and observe the wedding ceremony. So you could say, if you like, that this is my projection. And my dream, my malevolence, my . . . prophecy.

TK: My method of working on this performance can be reduced, more or less, to the following formula: everything is the same as it was before, the same characters, the same objects, the same words. But from all this "sameness" emerges something utterly, but utterly, different . . .

Notes

1 Kantor had lately become preoccupied with the idea of his group as a company of "strolling players" such as those that existed in medieval or Renaissance Europe.

2 Actually a Polish folk carol, which Chopin incorporates into his B minor Scherzo.

19

BETWEEN LOVE AND DEATH

(Kantor's Farewell, 15 December 1990)

A shepherd boy, brought to life from a picture by Wojtkiewicz, and a fair-haired girl dressed in white. A little lad going wild on a wooden horse tirelessly parades past his bride, who is dragged along by a witch of the kind depicted by Goya. These are the Matchmakers of Death, from the Cricotage *The Machine of Love and Death*.

A little lad in a kiddy-kart, traversing the entire space of the room twice, which the ghost of the dead man had crossed shortly before. And alongside him, the generals, scrambling from every corner of the room like cockroaches, circling round the bed of the dying man. This is the "kingdom of departed glory" from my review *Let the Artists Die!*

The groom all in white, trying to manage the complicated components of his outfit. Straps and braces, clasps and embroiderings. The suitcase gets in the way, and the mattress has to be prepared for the arrival of the bride. But it turns out that the bride, set down so solicitously on the mattress, is dead. This is the "image of nuptials" from my dramatic miniature, *Où Sont les Neiges d'Antan?*

The common skivvy from the mortuary clings immoveably to the priest's bed, which is just as immoveably guarded by the grandmother, who drives her off with a chamberpot. The skivvy is the photographer's widow, trying to take a picture. The memorial photograph is designed to immortalise the platoon of recruits setting off for the front. Does immortalise mean preserve, or kill? Her camera turns out to be a machine gun. This is the "memory framing machine" from *Wielopole, Wielopole*.

Standing in the corner of the classroom, the skivvy is loaded down with the tools of her trade. Among the brushes and the brooms, the shovels and the buckets, a great broom grows – which looks quite harmless for the time being. But it is this broom that turns the constantly repeated movements of cleaning into ritual gestures: the last rites of the weird inhabitants of *Dead Class*.

The thug, someone who terrifies with the rythmicality of his killing, a fascinating thug. Moreover he kills the woman he loves most. He makes a thorough job of it. He kills her because he loves her, because he will love her still. This is the first commandment of the "decalogue of love", the happening-style finale of *The Water Hen*.

People lose their heads when they're in love. Love, in fact, is so inexorable that you can even lose two heads. You just have to have two; and a man with two heads can occur in nature. But two heads are not enough if the bride – the "domestic hen", you might say (literally shut away in a hen-coop) leads in her wake a whole crowd of suitors. In that case, two heads aren't enough to spot the deception. That is rule number two in the "game of love", a fundamental tenet of the Impossible Theatre, and *Lovelies and Dowdies*.

Without the open space of the room, the wardrobe cramps the lovers' movements. "Hung up" like their clothing on coathangers, they take their chance of making contact with each other in material shape. Mixed up with objects, crumpled, they have recourse to the simplest forms of expression. Weeping, babbling, stammering, howling, sobbing, but also invective. Debauchery checks desire, bliss expires in excess, suffering subdues sinful acts. Love in the Informel Theatre was an opportunity to play with Witkacy, in *The Country House*.

Words, above all, hamper love, sentences encroach upon it, and phrases flatten it altogether. Poetic phrases, particularly. Love cannot endure game-playing, yet demands game-playing, though games are exhausting. Juggling with chance, dissolving logic, slowing the tempo, are a means of self-realisation. A means of annihilating one's own state, freezing it for a while, holding a cinematic "stop-frame". Unwillingness to play eliminates the text. The annihilation machine, which in this case, has taken on the form of a pile of chairs, interlinked and constantly in movement, are an aid to this manifestation of the Zero Theatre in *The Madman and the Nun*.

> If I turn my back on the artistic space constituted by the stage, what am I left with? I am left with the auditorium.

> Our past becomes a buried treasure we forget with time, where feelings, frozen frames, likenesses that once were so close to us, things, clothes, faces, and chance events are all scattered. Their deadness is a sham, you just have to set them in motion and they start to live in memory and interact with the present.

> The artist, who believes in art – or the inevitability of the unbroken development of art – must counterpose the moment, the hour, the situation in which we find ourselves, against all those which preceded it. Only then does the artist have real inspiration.

45. Tadeusz Kantor. Photo: Jacek Barcz

The beautiful is, for me, the harmony and variety of forms, values which give joy to life, the initiative and the mental strength of human beings.

Folk art only counts when it manages to cross its own national boundaries.

For me, theatre is the passageway through which the dead pass in order to enter our life.

Is it possible to make a proper love machine?
  No.
  What about a death machine?
  That's possible.

Questions and answers. Answers and questions. Creators of the true and the uncompromising. At the beginning and at the end of their art. Art which from 8 December on, is already history.

When I try to show people in a compressed form the evidence of everything I have discovered in the course of many years following the Master, I shall take care not to forget one characteristic utterance from the last stage of his artistic "games with death".

He said, just before the staging of his last play – with its provocative title *I'll Come Again No More*:

> I felt that she (i.e., Death) still has one more surprise in store for me, that she is preparing something exceptionally important, which will not let her rest. She has even abandoned her place behind the scenes. She has shown herself in the glare of the footlights in all her majesty, as if for her last struggle. I watched in consternation and despair. Because here she was, squaring up to her greatest rival – Love. Capricious love, the love which dies, squandered, and the love which remains and endures in calamity. To the very end. And that is when she appears, powerful, solitary, able to transform hopeless defeat into victory.

Looking ahead to his next quarter of a century in the title of his new première, *Today is my Birthday*, already almost finished after rehearsals in Kraków and Toulouse, Kantor failed to foresee one thing: that he would not be there himself . . .

AFTERWORD

Kantor's Ascension

The fact that in the history of painting there are twice as many instances of Assumptions as Ascensions must strike one as odd. Common sense, confronted by this heretical comparison, demands that we acknowledge the "normality" of these statistics. After all, it is easier to be "taken up" to Heaven than to climb up there. This would demand not just application and courage, but a creative miracle! Artists have sensed this more deeply than theologians. That's why they haven't chanced it. They haven't even chanced it in their creative output.

Kantor belonged to the company of artists who have carried the challenge – in our time known as the avant-garde – far beyond the bounds of artistic creation. In his passion to open up the frontiers of art and life Kantor discovered the sphere of existence which is normally called death. This sphere of "life after life" so fascinated the creator of the Theatre of Death, that he devoted seventeen years of his life to it. As an avant-gardist, determined to take first place in the ranks of artistic discoveries, he indisputably secured that place the moment he ceased to scamper after supremacy in the domain of outwardly impressive performances. *Dead Class* (1975) took every possible risk. The risk of stripping bare the face of an embattled avant-gardist. Embattled against the avant-garde. Embattled in the name of oneself and one's own art. The risk paid off, because the struggle turned into a discovery. The discovery of oneself as a human being and an artist at the same time.

The touchstone Kantor used to test his imagination in the ensuing Theatre of Death productions, *Wielopole, Wielopole, Let the Artists Die!* and *I'll Come Again No More*, and the handful of five-finger-exercise Cricotages that accompanied them – the most important of which was *Où Sont les Neiges d'Antan?* – led to a real tension in his work between Life and Death. Death as the *terminus e quo* of creativity. And as the *terminus ad quem*. Death as the be-all and end-all of creativity. Death as the basic *raison d'être* of art and as the sole motivating force on life's course. The condition of the Kantor actor had to be a living death for that reason.

Kantor took a stand against death, taunted her, defied her, associated with her on the most intimate terms. Associated with her rather like the Mexican tribes of Incas and Mayas, like the inhabitants of Honshu, like the Australian Aborigines fleeing from Captain Cook in the depths of the Red Desert. His last production, which bore the challenging, next-in-line title *Today Is My*

Birthday, was not just the high point on a road already travelled. Not just the "store of roads gone before", which accompanied him on his travels across five continents from 1969 onwards, that is, from the time he took his underrated happening-style *The Water Hen* to France and the British Isles. *Today is My Birthday* was an attempt at integration of theatre and painting. The Infanta, who left Velasquez's portrait for a while to inhabit Kantor's canvas, was to meet the Girl who Isn't Here on the Cricot stage: who in reality was Kantor's muse. The poor water-carrier from the village of Wielopole Skrzyńskie, at the foot of the hill, which once lay on the Amber Trail, must have been recognised by the canon-priest, Józef Śmietana. This was Kantor's contemporary, who presided over the return of the artist to the parish where he was born. The priest bent his knee every day in front of a portrait of his namesake, St Julian, painted by his friend "Tadzio" Kantor, who at the time was a student at the Kraków Academy of Fine Arts. A few months after Martial Law had been declared, Śmietana made the historic, maybe over-the-top comparison between Wielopole and the Hebrew settlement of Nazareth. The film also records the quasi-ritual proclamation of Jonasz Stern, "I wash his feet": Stern is a great artist who has never lost sight of his Jewish origins or communist beliefs.[1] Just as Maria Jaremianka, the true founder of Cricot 2 on the female side, has never forgotten. They were chosen by Kantor to bear witness to his way, as partakers of his birthday banquet. These, his friends, were given a present of no mean sort. The voice of the great artist Vsevolod Meyerhold,[2] whom the Stalinists left to rot, rang out like a pardon. A pardon for all those who, in the name of art, gave credence to totalitarianism. They believed, and they fell victim to it.

Kantor had invited everyone to his birthday party. All his characters and their doubles, all the grotesque marionettes and their human likenesses. The difference between the "stuffed people" and the representatives of the "special quality people" in power is the same as the difference between the NKVD people[3] and gravediggers. Regardless of whether they are urged to join the dance by the singing Beadle from *Dead Class*, or fiddled into it by Uncle Stasio coming back from the First World War in *Wielopole, Wielopole*. The news vendor from 1914 is the cue for the German hymn *Gott Erhalte, Gott Beschütze*. Prior to summoning the presence of the Father as he bids farewell to the Mother before leaving for the front, he encounters the inspired phantom of Dr Klein, the local Jehovah, preparing everyone in advance for the worst. Father, whom the son once hated (*Wielopole, Wielopole*), and then elevated to the altar of forgiveness (*I'll Come Again No More*), acquires his identical-twin shadows. The owner of "the poor" and "room of imagination" tries to hold on to two equally intriguing faces: one is his self-portrait, directly mimicking his gestures and mannerisms, and the other is his shadow, occupying the bed of death. The owner, however, who was to have been accompanied by the skivvy posing as a critic (a savage gift for the "trend-hounds" now licking dust from the Master's feet!) has not lived to see his dramatic birthday. He hasn't lived to see it, yet he has remained on stage. His partners in the play, which goes on still, never forget that he is present. It is good that they have not interrupted

46. Tadeusz Kantor. Photo: Jacek Barcz

the play in order to say: "Our dreams, thoughts, and deeds we offer to You." I'm sure they feel as I do, standing at your graveside:

"Tadeusz – you were the greatest artist of the Polish theatre. You didn't have to wait for your Assumption. You had ascended long since into the Heaven of Art."

Notes

1   Jonasz Stern (b.1904–1988) was a prominent painter and founder of the Grupa Krakowska (Kraków Group).
2   Vsevolod Meyerhold (1874–1940) is commonly set against Konstantin Stanislavsky (1863–1938), as if his fascination with the formal metamorphoses of theatrical space and the modalities of theatrical language (Formalism) were diametrically opposed to the older director's Naturalism. The truth (as usual) is more complex: but it is nevertheless true that Meyerhold, after being the doyen of avant-garde theatre, was arrested and murdered because his formalism was too radical for the party bosses.
3   The NKVD was one of the security organisations that preceded the KGB, responsible for the purges of the thirties.

POSTSCRIPT

Kantor's Theatre, without Kantor (1999)

Only a few years have passed since Kantor's tragic, somehow theatrical death, which compromised the company's very existence. The death of this man, whose life had been bound up with the Theatre of Death, happened suddenly, without warning.

Certain hostile elements condemned the "criminal practice of keeping his theatre alive" when the actors involved in Kantor's last production, *Today is my Birthday* undertook several world tours. In the West, the wave of opposition was spearheaded by the eminent French critic Guy Scarpetta, who upset everyone with the title of his anniversary piece, "Tadeusz Kantor's Second Death", as well as its key proposition, "You can't have the 'Kantor Theatre' without Kantor, and all these efforts at keeping it going are nothing less than pure fraudulence."

The production, meanwhile, after being premiered at Beaubourg (the Pompidou Centre) in Paris, toured most of the world's capitals and graced the Warsaw Drama Festival. Along with the actors, most of its reviewers sensed the urge "to bring the thing to fruition", which was only natural, and reinforced by the fact that the preparations for its opening had reached an advanced stage. This is indicated in a lecture by painter and actress Maria Stangret, Kantor's widow, and one of the two true heirs to his legacy:

> Once Krzysztof Miklaszewski said to Kantor: "Theatre is such an ephemeral genre, what do you think will become of your theatre in years to come? and Kantor answered on that occasion, "Yes, you're right. But Cricot's intellectual and artistic programme is exceptionally powerful, so I dream of its productions outliving me, because every true artist dreams of his art surviving his death." This was the mission he entrusted us with – I don't like the word "mission", it smacks of mysticism – anyway, that was his wish, and that is why the group is still performing.

In the same lecture on 27 January 1992 (a month and a half after Scarpetta's attack), and referring to the revival of *Dead Class*, Stangret added:

> Obviously, we are not going to just duplicate things, and even more important, there will not be a *continuation* of Kantor. That would be quite unacceptable.
>
> *Gazeta Wyborcza*, 1992, n. 22, p. 17

This marked the first schism in the group, because the actors supported Stangret's views, while Scarpetta's anathema lent credence to the "scholarly" position associated with Cricoteca, the Cricot 2 Theatre Centre which Kantor had envisioned as a "living archive and museum". Here, Anna Halczak, a close collaborator of the Master, stood in the forefront of those opposed to "copying" Kantor.

Over the years, the situation grew even more complex. Enthused by the success of theatrical copies (of Kantor), the actors formed two strongly contrasted groups. It was typical of Stangret that she was absent from both; together with her nephew, Leszek Stangret, she embarked upon the creation and support of domestic and overseas institutions whose task was defined as "safeguarding the memory of the life and creative work of Tadeusz Kantor". So the Tadeusz Kantor Fund came into being; while the Master's workshop, located in the bowels of the last apartment he was to live in, also sprang into life. Here, too, was born the idea of awarding an annual prize for artists in the name of Cricot 2; and firm foundations for the existence and development of the Cultural Centre/Maria and Tadeusz Kantor Museum were established in the village of Huciska (a sort of Polish Barbizon) in the Pogórze plateau outside Kraków. All these places and institutions are linked now by the activities of Cricoteca, which in addition to its headquarters at Kanonicza 5 in Kraków, has acquired such additional spaces as the Krzysztofory cellars, where from the time of *The Water Hen* (1967) onwards, Kantor's theatrical productions regularly took place.

In the meantime, Kantor's actors have gone their own way. The Janicki brothers, those much-loved identical twins, had formed the Twins Company as early as 1992, in the shape of a group operating both in Kraków and Milan. Along with two other actors who regularly appeared in Cricot 2 from 1981 onwards, Janusz Jarecki and Bogdan Renczyński, the Janicki brothers staged a production of Beckettiana, in which the two *Acts without Words* were presented alongside *Krapp's Last Tape*. The Janicki brothers did this as a way of underlining the autonomy of their work, even though it was based on the work of Kantor. This process recurred every so often from 1991 on: first of all in the context of the "Other Group", which they formed along with Jacek Stokłosa, and then on their own – a sort of painterly-theatrical intervention with exhibitions, happenings, incidents, events, and performance.

In May 1993, moreover, Andrzej Wełmiński gathered around him a number of people who worked at various times with Kantor. Among others these consisted of Mirosława Rychlicka, Teresa Wełmińska, Zbigniew Gostomski, Zbigniew Bednarczyk, Andrzej Kowalczyk, Stanisław Michno, the man who built the weird Kantor machines, Eugeniusz Bakalarz, and the loyal sound engineer, Krzysztof Dominik.

And while the Janickis' adoption of the uncontroversial sobriquet "The Twins" never provoked any special reaction, the other group's title, "Actors from the Cricot Theatre", gave rise to a stormy outburst. In 1994, in particular, an attack was mounted on the Wełmiński group from all sides: the widow from Cricoteca and the post-Kantor institutions, and all those former colleagues who had failed to be included in the new ensemble. The first production was *Maniacs*, inspired by Roman Jaworski's notorious avant-garde tale, *The Stories of the Maniacs*, a text which had long played in Poland, unacknowledged, a role resembling that of the short stories of Schulz.

Even more typical, and underlining the group's relation to the Kantor tradition, is the production's subtitle: *Their Master's Voice*. Andrzej Wełmiński gives the following interpretation:

Why *Maniacs*? It comes from "mania", the opposite of "technique" or "skill". "Mania" is the creative drive, while "technique" is related more to reproduction, craftsmanship, production. Besides, someone wrote that Wełmiński, with maniacal stubbornness, keeps trying to push his actors further, even though you can see from the outside that it's pointless, and can't possibly succeed . . . A section of the group has grasped the fact that it is in good shape, and can work and develop creatively, by handing on the heritage Kantor bequeathed to us.

Cultural News, 1994, nr. 4, p. 23, 19 June 1994

The reaction of the press and judgement of the fans were considerably more positive in the case of the Janicki brothers – "Beckett is a laugh. All credit to the Janickis, for showing us this" – than for the Wełmiński group:

This production . . . implodes . . . along the fault-lines of the characters Kantor once sketched out for us, who were closely identified forever after with particular actors; having been set in motion, these marionettes continue to operate within the spheres of their "trade".

Nevertheless, both groups appeared amicably together at the same national and international festivals. This is how the Spaniards, for instance, came to write:

The International Theatre Festival in Valladolid this week pays tribute to Tadeusz Kantor. The two groups known as "Twins Company" and "Actors from Cricot 2" discovered their own theatrical identity following the death of the great Polish avant-gardist.

El Mundo de Valladolid, 23 November 1993

In 1994, this idyll came to an end. From the middle of that year, everyone was working on their own. It was evident from the words of an impartial observer, however, that some kind of dialogue was still possible.

"Kantor's theatre after Kantor's death" – this was the topic of discussion between members of the group of artists who "came out" as the people who were entirely responsible for the art-work entitled *Dead Class*. This panel of experts could easily have ended up in an empty academic debate about the greatness of the Master. But it might also have gone in a quite different direction. It might have taken up the question of how Kantor conceived of theatre and how he experienced it – after all, he *was* a kind of one-man theatre of the independent avant-garde . . . But alas, it ended up in an hour-long slanging-match about how the Master's posthumous bequest ought to be divided up . . .

Paweł Głowacki, "State of Weightlessness",
Universal Weekly, 1994, nr. 18, p. 10

My responsibilities as a journalist force me to add that both the Janickis and the Wełmiński group are still operating, but that they now have absolutely no mutual contact, that the Italians from Florence who took part in Cricot 2 from the *Wielopole, Wielopole* rehearsals onwards have been wandering about all over Europe, that Roman Siwulak ran some rehearsals in France, that

Stanisław Rychlicki has appeared from time to time in little "alternative" youth theatres, and that Zofia Kalińska, who dropped Kantor's theatre as early as the *Dead Class* days, has been running her own author's theatre AKME with success – even with great success. Designated a "woman's theatre" (though this is a simplification), AKME performs regularly at international festivals, including Edinburgh. I have been working since 1988 (in other words, since leaving Cricot 2, and particularly in England) on the theory and practice of reconstructing Kantor's acting methods (New Method).

The dramatic struggles of Kantor's heirs prove that their reputation as puppets, deprived of all freedom in the hands of the man who created them, is a piece of second-hand mystification. The truth is quite otherwise. Not only did Kantor love his actors, and respect them, as well as hate them, as my documentaries revealed, Kantor also *worked* with his actors, quite simply. He worked long and hard with them. What is more he worked *consciously*, in contradistinction to what he said when trying to satisfy the public's insatiable curiosity about him. What is more, Kantor had a "method". A method which was very clear-cut and precise. A method which he never disclosed, expostulating at press conferences that his "school" had no interest for him. *He* was the "Kantor school", he said; his imagination, his unconscious, his performance, and . . . chance.

All this is both true and untrue. As the creator of the Cricot Dramatic Session, Kantor is truly a unique creative spirit. He didn't create just one particular sort of performance, or one identifiable form of theatre. Every scenic "proposition" has to be seen in the larger context of his entire creative output. You cannot detach it from the context. There is just one "but"; given that the Kantor theatre is founded upon a new concept of seeing, a *painterly* seeing, it is mediated through a conscious Man of the Theatre, who knows very well that the backbone of this vision will always be the actor.

To understand this and destroy the stereotypes, you have to look at the stubborn fight Kantor's actors put up in order to survive, and to take their place alongside Kantor in a New Way of Acting. But that is another story, or rather a subject for another book.

47. Tadeusz Kantor. Photo: Jacek Barcz

TADEUSZ KANTOR (1915–1990)

A Chronicle of his Life and Works
(Translated by Barbara Herchenreder)

6 April 1915
Birth of TADEUSZ KANTOR, son of Helena and Marian, in Wielopole
Skrzyńskie. Helena gives birth in the Catholic presbytery. Her maiden name
was Berger and she had lived here since her childhood, together with her wid-
owed mother, Katarzyna. Her mother was the step-sister of Father Józef
Radoniewicz, the parish priest and dean of Wielopole. The theme of the presbytery and its parish priest will appear in Kantor's play *Wielopole, Wielopole*
(1980).

15 October 1921
The death of Father Radoniewicz means Helena Kantor and her two children, Tadeusz and his older sister, Zofia, have to leave the presbytery. Having
become involved with another woman, their father had never returned to
Helena after the war. This theme of abandonment Kantor will also continue
to develop later in *Wielopole, Wielopole*.

1924
After the move to Tarnów, he starts school in the IV Class of the Training
School of the Men's Teacher Training College (he had already undergone
three years in Wielopole).

1925–1933
Kantor passes his matriculation examination and graduates from Kazimierz
Brodziński High School in Tarnów. During this period the young Kantor would
spend his school holidays in his home town of Wielopole. During the summer
of 1932 he makes friends with the young curate, Julian Śmietana, for whom he
will later carry out a series of painting commissions in the parish church.

5 October 1934
Kantor joins the Department of Painting at the Kraków Academy of Fine
Art, specifically the studio of Professor Władysław Jarocki. Kantor is fascinated by the work of Stanisław Wyspiański (d. 1907), who was closely
associated with Kraków. His high-school set design projects for the plays
Wyzwolenie (Liberation) and *Akropolis* (1932) are now followed by his set
design for the play *Sędziowie* (The Judges) (1935).

1937–1938

Kantor is captivated by the work of Maurice Maeterlinck. A student set-design project for the play *Interiors*, put on at the Academy of Fine Art's student halls of residence, is followed by his production of *The Death of Tintagiles* in the Marionette Theatre.

1937–1939

Whilst studying painting, Kantor also attends the classes of Professor Karol Frycz, the eminent set-designer, "citizen of the world", friend of Craig and of Stanislavsky, and director of Kraków theatres. Frycz conducts classes in decorative painting and set design at the Academy. Kantor attends evening classes in drawing held by the renowned caricaturist, Kazimierz Sichulski, as well as lectures and workshops in architecture. He follows a wide range of educational pursuits, studies under the foremost teachers and achieves the highest possible grades. When war breaks out he remains in Kraków, supplementing his income as a painter-decorator. On 12 December 1939 he takes his final examination with Professor Frycz.

1940–1942

The first years of the German occupation, Kantor spends like most Poles of Jewish extraction: he works as a labourer and hides out in the Wielopole area (it is then that he carries out works of painting in the Church in Nockowo near Wielopole). It is at this time that he receives news of the arrest of his father, Marian (8 December 1940), who is one of the first to be transported from Tarnów to Auschwitz, where he dies in the Auschwitz-Birkenau concentration camp on 1 April 1942.

1942–1944

Along with his friends from the Academy and other young, rebellious painters studying at the Kunstgewerbeschule (the only school of art, run by the German occupants, where Poles are "allowed" to study), Kantor sets up an underground Independent Theatre. Rehearsals take place in the home of Ewa Jurkiewicz, who was later to be Kantor's first wife. Kantor, fascinated by Aleksander Blok's *The Showman's Booth*, which he had translated back in 1938 together with Wanda Baczyńska, his "great student love", now wanted to stage this play by the avant-garde Russian writer. In late autumn he decides, however, to stage *Balladyna*, a "classical" Romantic play by Słowacki. The opening performance takes place in Ewa Siedlecka's apartment on 22 May 1943. Siedlecka's apartment is deemed safe as her father, the eminent ethnologist, Professor Siedlecki, holds honorary doctorships of all the German universities. This group of young artists, which includes Poland's future foremost painters (Tadeusz Brzozowski, Jerzy Nowosielski, Kazimierz Mikulski), set-designers (such as Jerzy Skarżyński), art critics (Mieczysław Porębski) and journalists (Jerzy Turowicz), embark on a second underground production, of *The Return of Odysseus* (first night on 22 July 1944). This time the performance takes place in the apartment belonging to Professor Tadeusz Stryjeński, the renowned architect, who had also been honoured by the Germans and was therefore under less suspicion.

1945
Kantor takes up the position of Director of the Painting Department in the Stary Theatre in Kraków and, at the same time, signs up for a set-design course in the newly formed Studio Teatralne (Theatrical Studio) run by Andrzej Pronaszko, of whom Kantor wrote: 'while Frycz, my professor in the Academy, represented the Craig School, Pronaszko was a radical constructivist. Frycz created unforgettable ambiances. Pronaszko taught methods and constructions." On 17 June 1945, Kantor made his debut as a set designer in the professional theatre (with a play by Zofia Nałkowska entitled *Dzień Jego Powrotu* (The Day of His Return)). Kantor creates set designs for several plays that year and becomes noted for his innovative approach (mobile sets, puppets, grotesque forms). At the same time he takes part in the first post-war exhibition of the *Grupa Młodych Plastyków* (Young Artists Group).

18 November 1946
Together with Maria Jarema, Kantor (as the first of two Polish painters) takes part in the International Exhibition of Modern Art at the Paris Musée d'Art Moderne. The journey to France by way of Switzerland is eventful, as here Kantor discovers "the freedom of the imagination", represented on the one part by the surrealists and, on the other, by Matta and Tanguy.

1947–1948
Appointed Professor of Painting in the Wyższa Szkoła Sztuk Plastycznych (University College of Art and Design) in Kraków, Kantor commences by attacking "Obscurantism and Traditionalism" and then goes on to take part in all possible exhibitions of new art forms (Warsaw, New York and Kraków, where the first Exhibition of Modern Art was opened on 19 December 1948).

1949
The political authorities commence attacks on the new art forms. They adopt Soviet "precepts of Socialist Realism" as the compulsory form in Polish art. This means the demise of the Exhibition of Modern Art and the end of Kantor's career as a teacher.

1950
Dismissed from the college, Kantor is employed by the State Dramatic Theatres as a set designer. He mainly works in the Stary Theatre (up to 1961). Initially slated for his "formalism", he is hailed as one of the "most creative set-designers", particularly after the October 1956 revolution. His designs are said to be dynamic sets, serving as "an example of a benign creative encroachment on a theatrical performance. The artist is interested in the relationship between space, objects, the actor and the text in a situation where all these elements exist independently of each other on the stage." This understanding of the role of an artist could only end in separation from the institutional

theatre, despite the fact that, since 1956, Kantor had been very well received and had created several dozen set-designs, mainly in Kraków.

1955

This is a momentous year for Kantor who, as a member of the famed "ten" Polish artists, had protested against Socialist Realism as far back as 1949 and had paid the price of his actions. The Kraków exhibition of works by nine artists (T. Brzozowski, M. Jarema, *T. Kantor*, J. Maziarska, K. Mikulski, J. Nowosielski, E. Rosenstein, J. Skarżyński and J. Stern), held in the Dom Plastyków on 13 December, heralds the return of modern art to Poland. It also heralds the setting up of the "Grupa Krakowska" (Kraków Group), an association of artists working in the new art forms. That autumn, too, Maria Jarema, together with Kantor and Kazimierz Mikulski, sets up the Cricot 2 Theatre, whose name goes back to the pre-war "Cricot" artistic theatre (1933–1939), which had been established by Jarema's older brother, Józef, and Władysław Józef Dobrowolski (an uncle of the author of this book – Krzysztof Miklaszewski).

In 1955 Kantor visits Paris and publishes his *Parisian Notes*, in which he foretells the coming of *informel* drama form, inspired by French *art informel*.

12 May 1956

The premiere of *Mątwa* (*Cuttlefish*) (directed by Kantor, costumes: M. Jarema) inaugurates the activities of the Cricot 2 Theatre, thus continuing the tradition of the Cricot Theatre, which had also begun its activities in 1933 with this play by Stanisław Ignacy Witkiewicz (known as Witkacy) and which – in the words of Kantor – "was a rebellion against the official theatre which was ruled by false pathos, worthless bombast and self-conceit". This "commedia dell'arte in abstracto" heralds the beginning of "Kantor's play with Witkacy" which was to last from 1956 to 1975 and which would be characterised by a personal interpretation of Witkiewicz's plays which, to Kantor, were merely a starting point, a base for his own show.

1957–1961

Kantor is simultaneously involved in a wide range of activities: as a painter he travels and works in Poland and abroad, presenting several one-man exhibitions (Stockholm, Paris, Düsseldorf, New York, Göteborg); as a set designer for the Stary Theatre, co-founder of the Cricot 2 Theatre and, as an organiser of Poland's artistic circles, he becomes the first chairman of the Kraków Group of Artists and formulates his own Tachism programme. This is his third attempt – following on from the "metaphorical pictures" of the 1950s – at "rescuing and preserving matter", which – as he explained in his *Notatnik 55* (*55 Notes*) – "is subject to a continuous process of decay".

At this time, too, the Cricot 2 Theatre, which Kantor runs single-handedly following the death of Jarema (1 November 1958), embarks on a new era in its activities, as the Informel Theatre. Its crowning glory is the première of *W Małym Dworku* (*The Country House*), based on a play by Witkacy (14 January 1961). The mutual dependency of theatre and of art is best described by Kantor himself: "Painting need not be confined exclusively to picturization – I want to carry it through into *space* and *time*, *by means of people* who move within them."

1961–1964

While continuing his painting activities abroad (a new exhibition in Paris, a second one in New York, teaching stints in the Academy of Fine Art in Hamburg, journeys to Italy and Sweden), in Poland Kantor sets up a much publicised Popular Exhibition which takes up all the cellar space of the Kraków Krzysztofory Gallery (30 November – 15 December 1963).

In its *Manifest* he wrote: "I am organising the first anti-exhibition, thus negating the concept of a "closed" and completed work; I am changing the attitude and perception of the viewer, as well as the status of a work of art, opening it up to the environment".

This attitude is further emphasised by the *Manifest – Zero* and the inception of the Teatr Zerowy (Zero Theatre), exemplified in particular by the première of Witkiewicz's play *Wariat i Zakonnica* (The Madman and the Nun) (8 June 1963).

It is at this time, too, that the first form of "amballages" (packaging) appears – envelopes and letters stuck onto canvasses of various sizes.

In Switzerland, Kantor announces his *Manifest – Amballage*, then presents his first paintings with amballages and the first umbrellas incorporated into a picture: "Through the medium of amballage, I created a portrait of the person most dear to me – my mother – from her youth to her death," wrote Kantor after the death of Helena Kantor (17 March 1962).

1965–1972

The year 1965 begins with Kantor's visit to the USA, together with Maria Stangret (whom he married in Paris on 10 April 1961) and ends with the first "happening" to be organised in Poland by the creator of amballage, entitled "Cricotage". This marks the beginning of Kantor's relationship with Warsaw's Galeria Foksal, run by Wiesław Borowski, Anna Ptaszkowska and Mariusz Tchorek (10 December 1965). The cycle of "happenings", both foreign (Basle: *Le Grand Emballage* – transmitted throughout Switzerland, 1966: Nüremberg – *Encounters with a Rhinoceros* – 1968 and *Anatomy Lesson according to Rembrandt* – 1968, repeated later in Dourdan – 1971 and Oslo – 1971, Bled – eight events) and Polish (the most famous was *The Letter* in the Foksal Gallery – 1967; *A Panoramic Sea Happening* in Osieki on the Baltic coast, in which 1600 people took part – 1967 and *Hommage á Maria Jarema* – 1968) is supported by the showing of *Kurka Wodna* (*The Water Hen*) by Witkiewicz (première on 28 April 1967), acknowledged by Kantor as an example of the Theatre of Happenings.

The series of foreign exhibitions is accompanied by a number of prestigious awards given to Kantor (the second prize for painting at the ninth Biennale in Sao Paulo in 1967, the European Premio Marzotto award for painting in 1968), while German Saarbrücken Television screens two documentary films (*The Journey* and *Kantor ist da*). At this time, too, *Kurka Wodna* is the first of

Kantor's plays to be staged at prestigious European theatrical festivals (Rome – Premio Roma, 1969; Nancy – 1971; Edinburgh – 1972), and thus heralds the beginning of the international successes of Cricot 2.

In the late 60s and early 70s, Kantor comes up with the concept of an Impossible Statue – a colossal concrete "Chair", a monumental sculpture. The idea of transposing an ordinary chair, devoid of any aesthetic value, and placing an enormous copy of it in an open-air exhibition is carried out twice: in Vela Luka in Yugoslavia (August–September 1968) and in Oslo, near the Sonja Hennie–Niels Onstad Kunstsenter Museum (8 December 1971).

The "Chair" would be put up a third time, in Poland, in 1995 on the fifth anniversary of the death of Kantor. It was erected thanks to the Kantor Foundation near his Home/Museum in Huciska, where it stands to this day.

A sour note in Kantor's life is sounded when he is once again stripped of the position of Professor in the Kraków Academy of Fine Art, following the "March purges" of 1968.

1973–1975

The exhibition of painting entitled *Wszystko Wisi Na Włosku* (Everything Hangs by a Hair) is memorable in that it returns to the concept of a "closed" work of art (10 March 1973, at the Galeria Foksal in Warsaw); it is accompanied in 1973 by a new Cricot 2 première, *Lovelies and Dowdies* (4 May 1973 – Krzysztofory Gallery in Kraków) – a manifestation of the Impossible Theatre. It is at this time, too, that the first Polish documentary film about Kantor's theatre is shown. This was Miklaszewski's *Tadeusz Kantor's Cloakroom*, which endeavours to show the birthing process of a play.

The years 1973 and 1974 see a triumphal tour of *Lovelies and Dowdies* through world-class festivals (Edinburgh, Glasgow – 1973, Paris, Nancy, Rome, Shiraz and Essen – 1974).

1975–1979

The rehearsals of the "gripping séance", *Dead Class*, which had started in January 1975, finally came to fruit in a première held in the Krzysztofory Gallery in Kraków on 15 November 1975, along with the opening performances of *Dead Class* and "Theatre of Death".

Dead Class, which immediately stages several dozen performances in Kraków, proves a turning point, not only in Kantor's creativity but also in the way he is perceived. A six-week tour of England, Scotland and Wales in 1976 heralds the international success of this play. Following the performances in Britain, *Dead Class* is subsequently shown in 1977 in Holland, Germany, France, Iran, Yugoslavia, France once again, then Belgium; this is followed by 1978 by Italy, Australia, Switzerland. Then on to Venezuela, once again Italy, West Berlin, a further performance in Germany. And in 1979 – USA, Mexico, Italy once more, and Sweden.

Several hundred performances of *Dead Class* around the world make it the most internationally popular avant-garde play and, having already carried away prizes in Edinburgh in 1976, this premier position is crowned by the New York Critics Award OBIE 1979.

Kantor, in the meantime, continues his painting activities and exhibits worldwide (Stockholm, London (Whitechapel), Oslo, Kassel ("Documenta 6"), Rome and Milan. In Basle, he is awarded the Goethe Foundation's Rembrandt Prize.

On 27 January 1979, the Cricotage *Where are the Snows of Yesteryear?* has its first performance, alongside the exhibition *Cricot 2: Theatre and Artists in the Realms of Theatre*, held in the Pallazzo delle Esposizioni in Rome.

1980–1984

The allocation of premises at Kanoniczna 5 by the authorities of the City of Kraków leads to the setting up of the Cricoteca – a vibrant museum of Kantor's work. A cloned version is opened by the authorities of the City of Florence in Cricot 2's new home in Florence – the one-time Church of Santa Maria di Firenze. Here, in October 1979, Kantor embarks on rehearsals for a new play. On 23 June 1980, the première of *Wielopole, Wielopole* takes place, performed by Cricot 2, with the participation of Italian students. The show is financed by the Teatro Regionale Toscano and the authorities of the City of Florence. The first Polish showing takes place in the Sokół Hall in Kraków on 15 November 1980.

Wielopole, Wielopole is the second play in the Theatre of Death and gains immediate fame and recognition worldwide. In 1980 the world tour commences with Edinburgh and London, then moves on to Kraków, Warsaw and to Gdańsk, which is in the throes of the Solidarity revolution, and subsequently arrives in Paris. The following year – 1981 – begins with an Italian tour (Milan, Rome, Florence, Genoa, Parma), followed by Switzerland, Germany, Spain. The 1982 programme takes in Mexico, the United States and France. 1983 sees a tour of Spain and then finally, after performances in Kraków, *Wielopole, Wielopole* ends up in its native Wielopole. All this against a seething backdrop of martial law. The year 1984 takes performances of *Wielopole, Wielopole* to Sweden, Finland and once again to Spain and then, as the sole Polish entrant, to the pre-Olympic Festival of Art in Los Angeles. It is noteworthy that Cricot 2 was the only artistic ensemble from the so-called socialist bloc to take part in activities in Los Angeles, the Games having been boycotted by Russia and the Communist countries. In Los Angeles, Cricot 2 presents both *Wielopole, Wielopole* and *Dead Class*, which is still very much in demand. This is, however, the first instance where Kantor abandons a previous show, following the première of a new one. *Dead Class* was still played and not just in Poland. After Florence (1980) and Kraków (1981), it reappears in 1982 in Japan and in the Riverside Studios at Hammersmith, in London (17–28 January).

Kantor then wanders from country to country, avoiding Poland, which was under martial law, and during this period he renews the second version of the Cricotage *Where are the Snows of Yesteryear?* November 1982), in London (30 November – 5 December 1982), Geneva (1983) and, finally, Warsaw (1984).

1985–1987

The year 1985, which sees Kantor honoured with the French Légion d'Honneur in February, then sees a performance of *Let the Artists Die!* in the Alte Giesserei Kabelmetall in Nüremberg, thanks to financial co-operation with the Institut für Moderne Kunst in Nüremberg and the Centro di Richerche Teatrali in Milan. The same year it is produced, apart from Nüremberg and Milan, the spectacle is successfully repeated in Avignon, Paris and New York. The first Polish performance takes place in 1986 in Warsaw (11 January) and then, by way of Kraków, returns to Italy (Milan, Turin), France (Lyon, Grenoble), West Berlin and Belgium. In 1987, Kantor's "revue" *Niech szczezną artyści! (Let the Artists Die!)* is seen by Poles, Spaniards, Austrians, Italians, the French and Argentinians.

Increasingly, retrospective performances were being produced (Bari), often accompanied by a symposium on Kantor's artistic forms (Katowice and Antwerp). Kantor also puts on two Cricotages: in 1986 – *The Wedding* (Un matrimonio), presented in conjunction with students of the Scuola d'Arte Dramatica at the Piccolo Teatro in Milan and, in 1987, *The Machine of Love and Death* as part of the *Documenta 8* in Kassel, in Germany. These events are accompanied by lectures and publications (*Lezioni Milanesi*).

A particularly notable artistic event of this period was an exhibition *School Classroom – a Closed Work* (Cricoteka, Kraków, 1985), which had already been shown in Paris at the Pompidou Centre during an exhibition entitled "Présences Polonaises", which demonstrated clearly how Kantor's theatrical sets were an art form in themselves.

The mid 1980s saw a considerable proliferation of documentaries on Kantor's theatrical and artistic forms. Apart from films made by Denis Bablet, *The Theatre of Tadeusz Kantor* (CNRS, Paris) and Andrzej Sapija *Teatr Cricot 2* (WFO Łódź), Interpress Film Warszawa produced two documentaries made by Miklaszewski: *Let the Artists Die! (An Anatomy of Performance –* 1985) and *I – The Master* (a psychological portrait of the artist, which won a number of awards at festivals – 1986), the Kraków Television Centre produced two invaluable films from the series: *Kantor – My History of Art –* the first about Jacek Malczewski (1985) and the second about Witold Wojtkiewicz (1986) (written and produced by Miklaszewski).

The Barbican Art Gallery commissions a film entitled *Kantor on Malczewski – a Personal Vision*, written by Miklaszewski, and this accompanies an exhibition in the Barbican of Malczewski's paintings.

1988–1990

Rehearsals in Kraków and Milan of a German-Italian-French co-production (Berlin Kulturstadt, Centro di Ricerche Teatrali of Milan and Centre Pompidou of Paris) culminate in the premier of *Nigdy tu już nie powrócę (I'll Come Again No More)* in the Piccolo Teatro Studio in Milan (23 November 1988). The tours of this fourth play in the Theatre of Death series begin in the Akademie der Kunste in West Berlin on 20 May 1988 and finish in Reykyavik City Centre on 8 June 1990. There are further revues of Kantor's works (Paris 1989) and international symposia (Paris 1989, Kraków 1990). Kantor begins work on another Cricotage (1988 – *Un très courte leçon* (A Very Short Lesson)) at the Institut International de la Marionnette in Charleville-Meziers; 1990 – *O Douce Nuit* (Quiet Night) – Académie Experimentale des Théâtres d'Avignon). Kantor's theoretical works and manifestos appear in Italian, French and German. Beginning with an exhibition of seven of his newest paintings in the series *Dalej Już Nic* . . . (Nothing Further . . .) (5 March 1988), Kantor continues to exhibit his works in Paris, Berlin, Rome, Kraków and Wrocław.

For his contribution to the development of modern art, Kantor receives the highest awards and accolades of many countries (Poland's National Award First Class, the French Commandeur le l'Ordre des Arts et Lettres, the Federal German Republic's Grand Cross of Merit and the Italian Prix Pirandello).

Throughout 1990, intensive rehearsals of the play *Today is My Birthday* take place with occasional breaks, in Toulouse and in Kraków.

8 December 1990
Tadeusz Kantor dies suddenly in Kraków after an evening rehearsal of *Today is my Birthday*. The première of his unfinished play takes place in Toulouse at the Garonne Theatre on 10 January 1991 and in Paris at the Centre Georges Pompidou on 21 January 1991.

TADEUSZ KANTOR

World Bibliography

Selected texts of Tadeusz Kantor (in chronological order)

Surrealizm, "Przekrój", Kraków 1948, V

Cricot 2, "Życie Literackie", Kraków 1956, nr 20

Teatr zerowy/Le Théâtre de Zero, "Galeria Krzysztofory", Kraków 1963

Ambalaże, Staatliche Kunsthalle Baden-Baden, Baden-Baden 1966

Emballage-multiple, Galeria Foksal, Warszawa 1966

List, Galeria Foksal, Warszawa 1967

Panoramiczny happening morski, Koszalińskie Towarzystwo Społeczno-Kulturalne, Koszalin 1967

Du Théâtre de conspiration aux Emballages, Cricot 2, "Opus International", Paris 1968, nr 6

Il Teatro Cricot 2, "Leçon d'anatomie d'après Rembrandt", Partition-happening, "Grammatica 3", Roma 1969, VII

A propos de la "Boule d'eau" . . . , Galeria Krzysztofory, Kraków 1995–9

A proposito della "Gallinella", Manifesto del Teatro Zero, "Sipario", Milano 1969, nr 277, III

Multipart, Galeria Foksal, Warszawa 1970

Cambriolage, Galeria Foksal, Warszawa 1971

A propos d'un bilan qu'on avait convenu de ne pas faire, "International Theatre Information", Paris 1972, winter–spring

Happeningi, "Dialog", Warszawa 1972, nr 9

La condition d'acteur, Naissance du Théâtre Cricot 2, "Travail théâtral Lausanne", 1972, nr 6, I–III

"Les Cordonniers" de Witkiewicz, "Les Lettres Françaises", Paris 1972, nr 11

Partition: "Les Mignons et les Guenons" – Les Extraits, Théâtre National de Chaillot, Paris 1974

Zierpuppen und Schlampuppen – Texte, Folkwang Museum Essen, 1974

Le Théâtre de la Mort, edited by Denis Bablet, L'Age d'Homme, Lausanne 1977/second edition 1985

Ma voie vers le théâtre de la mort, "Annuaire International du Théâtre '78", Warszawa 1978

Il Teatro della Morte, edited by Denis Bablet, Ubulibri, Edizioni il Formichiere, Milano 1979/second edition 2000

Intermediaries between the living and dead/Médiateurs entre les vivants et les morts, "Theatre International" London 1981, nr 2

Reinventar la Vanguardia, "Pipirijaina", Madrid 1981, nr 19–20, X

Wielopole, Wielopole: Dramma e spettacolo di Tadeusz Kantor, edited by Roberto Agostini, Ubulibri, Milano 1981

Cricot 2. Immagini di un Teatro, Citazioni e disegni di Tadeusz Kantor, Le Parole Gelate, Roma 1982

Kantor's Theatre of Emotions – Texts by Tadeusz Kantor, "Studio International", London 1982, nr 993–994, vol. 195

Metamorphoses, Sté Nlle des Éditions du Chêne, Paris 1982

Où sont les neiges d'antan?, "Théâtre Public", Gennevilliers 1982, nr 48, XI–XII

Cricotage "Où sont les neiges d'antan?", "Rivista di Literature Moderne e Comparate", Milano 1983, vol. XXXVII, 3

Theater des Todes. Die Tote Klasse. Wielopole-Wielopole, edited by K. Günther Künnel and Barbara Ziegler, Verlag für moderne Kunst, Zirndorf 1983

Le Théâtre de la mort, Parco Picture Backs, Tokyo 1983

Metamorfozy, "Twórczość", Warszawa 1983, nr 5

El teatro de la muerte, edited by Kive Staiff, Ediciones de la Flor, Buenos Aires 1984/2nd edition – 1987

Wielopole, Wielopole, edited by Barbara Borowska, Wydawnicłwo Literackie, Kraków 1984

Die Tiefe Spur. Ein "Schluss"-Wort, "Mitteilungen des Instituts für moderne Kunst", Nürnberg 1985, nr 36/37/38, IX–X

The Writings of Tadeusz Kantor 1956–1985, "The Drama Review", New York 1986, vol. 30, nr 3

Írásai (his writings): *Credo, Halálszinház* (Theatre of Death) and *Akét* (The Double), "Kultúra és közösség", Budapest 1987, nr 1

Textos. Nuremberg 1985, "La ría del ocio", Bilbao 1987, nr 1, V

Dalej już nic. Cricoteka, Kraków 1988

Tadeusz Kantor. Ein Reisender – Seine Texte und Manifeste. Verlag für moderne Kunst Nürnberg, Nürnberg 1988

I Shall Never Return: A Manifesto. "Soviet and East-European Drama, Theatre and Film", New York 1988, vol. 8, nr 1, V

Lezioni Milanesi I: Scuola Elementare del Teatro, Ubulibri, Milano 1988

Mrtvi razred "15 Dana", Zagreb 1988, nr 4–5

Rencontres avec la Mort, "Théâtre Public", Gennevilliers 1988, Vol. 84, nr 11–12, XI–XIII

La dictadura es útil en el arte, "El Periódico de Cataluña", Barcelona 1989, nr 2

La Machine de l'Amour et de la Mort. Synopsis du cricotage, "Puck", Paris 1989, nr 2

Moje spotkania ze śmiercią, "Życie Literackie", Kraków 1989, nr 42

Smrt i teatar, "Scena", Novi Sad 1989, nr 5, IX–X

Une très courte leçon. Partition du cricotage, "Puck", Paris 1989, nr 2

Wielopole, Wielopole: An Exercise in Theatre, edited and translated by G. M. Hyde and Mariusz Tchorek, Marion Boyars, London 1990

Leçons de Milan, Actes Sud-Papiers, Paris 1990

Geijutsuka Jo, Kutabare, Sakuhinsha, Tokyo 1990

Opere dal 1956 al 1990, Spicchi dell'Est, Galleria d'Arte, Roma 1990

La mia opera – il mio viaggio, Commento intimo, edited by Meda Federica Motta, Editore S.n.A., Milano 1991

Lekcje mediolańskie. Edited by Anna Halczak, Cricoteka, Biuro Kongresowe miasta Krakowa, Kraków 1991

Ma création, mon voyage: commentaires intimes, Éditions Plume, Paris 1991

Memory, "Soviet and East-European Performance", New York 1991, nr 11

Tadeusz Kantor en het Circus van de Dood: Teksten over onafhan – kelijk theater,

International Theatre and Film Books, Amsterdam 1991

Testament et amour, "Alternatives théâtrales 37", Odéon-Théâtre de l'Europe, Bruxelles 1991, nr 37, V

Un'esistenza alla frontiera fra la vita e l'arte, "Invarianti" Roma 1991, R.V, nr 17–18

Hommage à Tadeusz Kantor, Zuhause, Mitteilungen des Instituts für moderne Kunst Nürnberg

A Journey Through Other Spaces: Essays and Manifestos, 1944–1990. With a Critical Study of Tadeusz Kantor's Theatre, Michał Kobiałka, University of California Press: Berkeley, Los Angeles, London 1993

My Creation, My Journey, Sezon Museum of Art, Tokyo 1994

Halālszinhāz. Irāsok a müvészetröl és a színházról. Edited by Laszlo Beke and Nina Király, MASZK, Budapest-Szeged 1994

El teatro de la muerte y el amor, Creador. La necesidad de la transmisión, "Creacion", Madrid 1995, nr 14, V

Tadeusz Kantor, L'Escena Memória/La Escena de la Memoria, Fundacio Caixa de Catalunya, Fundación Arte y Technologia, I Éscena de la Men, Barcelona, Madrid 1997

Szewcy/partytura, "Didaskalia", Kraków 1997, nr 22, XII

Kantor: Lisverk, Marionettmuseet, Stockholm 1998

Tadeusz Kantor: Z Archiwum Galerii Foksal, Galeria Foksal, Warszawa 1998

Metamorfozy: Teksty o latach 1938–1974, edited by Krzysztof Pléśniarowicz, Cricoteka, Księgarnia Akademicka, Kraków 2000

Books about Tadeusz Kantor's art (in chronological order)

Borowski, Wiesław: *Tadeusz Kantor*, Wydawnictwa Artystyczne i Filmowe, Warszawa 1982

Bablet, Denis/editor and author/: *Tadeusz Kantor. Les Voies de la Création Théâtrale*, Vol. XI, Éditions du Centre National de la Recherche Scientifique, Paris 1983/2d edition – 1990

Miklaszewski, Krzysztof: *Spotkania z Tadeuszem Kantorem*, Krajowa Agencja Wydawnicza, Kraków 1989

Pleśniarowicz, Krzysztof: *Teatr Śmierci Tadeusza Kantora*, Verba, Chomotów 1990

Banu, Georges/editor: *Kantor, L'Artiste du XXe Siècle*, Actes Sud-Papiers, Paris 1990

Kłossowicz, Jan: *Tadeusz Kantor*, Teatr, Państwowy Instytut Wydawniczy, Warszawa 1991

Miklaszewski, Krzysztof: *Spotkania z Tadeuszem Kantorem*, TKECh, Kraków 1992

Bablet, Denis/editor and author: *Tadeusz Kantor. 2. Les Voies de la Création Théâtrale*. Vol. XVIII, Paris 1993

Liceranzu, Jose Antonio Martinez: *El lugar del objeto en la obra de Tadeusz Kantor: Wielopole, Wielopole*, Argitarapen Zerbitzua Euskal Heerriko Unibersitatae, Leioa/Bizkais/1994

Pleśniarowicz, Krzysztof: *The Dead Memory Machine, Tadeusz Kantor's Theatre of Death*, Cricoteka, Kraków 1994

Pleśniarowicz , Krzysztof: *Teatr Nie-ludzkiej formy*, Universitas, Kraków 1994

Kłossowicz, Jan: *Tadeusz Kantors Theater*, A. Francke Verlag Tübingen und Basel, Tübingen 1995

Rosenzviag, Marcos: *El teatro de Tadeusz Kantor. El uno y el otro*, Editorial Leviatán, Buenos Aires 1995

Skiba-Lickel, Aldona: *Aktor według Kantora*, Zakład Narodowy im. Ossolińskich, Wrocław 1995

Buscarino, Maurizio: *Kantor. Cyrk śmierci/Kantor, Zirkus des Todes*, Sturzflüge Edition, Bozen 1997

Kott, Jan: *Kadysz. Strony o Tadeuszu Kantorze*, Wydawnictwo słówo obraz terytoria, Gdańsk 1997

Pleśniarowicz, Krzysztof: *Kantor. Artysta końca wieku*, Wydawnictwo Dolnośląskie, Wrocław 1977

Porębski, Mieczysław: *Deska. T. Kantor*, Wydawnictwo Murator, Warszawa 1997

Gryglewicz, Tomasz/editor: *W cieniu krzesła. Malarstwo i sztuka przedmiotów Tadeusza Kantora*, Universitas, Kraków 1997

Wiewióra, Dietmar: *Materie, kollektive Erinnerung und individuelle Existenz im Theater von Tadeusz Kantor, 1983–1991*, Universitas, Kraków 1998

Piskorz, Marta, Stangret, Lech/editor: *Dom twórczości Tadeusza Kantora i Marii Stangret-Kantor*, Fundacja im. T. Kantora, Kraków 1999

Bystydzieńska, Grażyna, Harris, Emma/editors: *From Norwid to Kantor. Essays on Polish Modernism dedicated to Professor G. M. Hyde.* Among articles – essay of Krzysztof Miklaszewski: *The actor in Kantor's theatre*, Wydawnictwa Uniwersytetu Warszawskiego, Warszawa 1999

Kott, Jan: *Kaddish. Pages sur Tadeusz Kantor*, Le Passeur, Actes Sud, Arles 2000

Scarpetta, Guy: *Kantor au présent. Une longue conversation*, Actes Sud, Arles 2000

Miklaszewski, Krzysztof: *Les Métamorphoses de Moi, Tadeusz Kantor ou La Vie par L'Art*, K Films Éditions, Paris 2001

AUTHORS AND THEIR WORKS

(excluding Tadeusz Kantor's work)

INDEX OF NAMES